TRADE UNIONS IN THE NEW SOCIETY

TRADE UNIONS
in the New Society

BY HAROLD J. LASKI

*(The substance of this book derives from
The Sidney Hillman Lectures for 1949)*

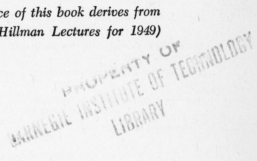

New York   1949
THE VIKING PRESS

TO THE MEMORY OF

SIDNEY HILLMAN, A GREAT LEADER AND A GREAT FRIEND

CONTENTS

PREFACE

THESE pages are the substance of the Sidney Hillman Lectures which I delivered in the United States during March-April 1949. I was greatly honored by the invitation of the Sidney Hillman Foundation to do so, and by the unfailing generosity and kindness that I received at its hands. I should like, in particular, to thank the director of the Foundation, Mr. Stuart Meacham, for an almost overwhelming sacrifice of his own time and effort in organizing the somewhat complex program the lectures involved. If I had not discovered that this is the form his friendship takes, I should have felt embarrassed by his unceasing devotion, especially as I knew how small was the hope that I could repay it. But I discovered rapidly that, with him, as with his colleagues in the Amalgamated Clothing Workers of America, friendship means service to the stranger. To him, to Mr. Jacob Potofsky, the president of the Union, and to Mr. Brandwen, its trusted counselor, I can only express my gratitude.

I owe, too, my thanks to Professor Schuyler Wallace of Columbia University, to the authorities at Howard, North Carolina, Roosevelt College, Denver, Harvard, and the New School for Social Research, for the way in which they made a heavy task easier by their friendly hospitality. I should like, too, to express my special thanks to Dean McHenry of the University of California at Los Angeles for the kind of courage in a difficult situation before which one can only be humble. To the members of the Amalgamated wherever I went I can say only that they acted toward me in the spirit of the great founder of their union.

This short book is, of course, only the briefest of preludes to its subject; I am well aware that it would need far more extensive treatment to set these problems in their full proportion and perspective. But when the Hillman Foundation asked me to deliver lectures in honor of Sidney Hillman, I thought of a friendship which went back to the days when I was a young instructor in Harvard, and he was already the most imaginative trade-union leader of his time. I learned much from him during the next thirty years; and the dedication of these pages to him is not only a personal word of thanks, but a tribute to one who made one of the vital, if inadequately recognized, contributions to the great effort which, after Pearl Harbor, made America that arsenal of democracy without which, as Marshal Stalin has himself admitted, the United Nations would have lost the Second World War.

HAROLD J. LASKI

The London School of Economics and Political Science

TRADE UNIONS IN THE NEW SOCIETY

I. THE CHANGING SIGNIFICANCE OF TRADE UNIONISM

1

IT IS not surprising that a crisis in our civilization should compel an effort to reassess the place of trade unions in the modern state. In the period between 1914 and 1945—almost exactly a generation—the facts of daily life have set all our major habits and institutions in a new perspective. In 1914 there was no Soviet Russia. In 1914 there was no expectation of full employment. In 1914 social insurance had not even begun to assume its present proportions. In 1914 the range of mass production and the speed of technological change had but little of the width and intensity they have come to possess. In 1914 there was nothing which even approached the degree to which peace is a function of increasing productivity, which, in its turn, is dependent upon the development everywhere of increased purchasing power. In 1914 the belief in a planned economy was confined to a small group of social philosophers whose heresies were treated with a mixture of amusement and contempt. Nor, in 1914, had the incisive genius of Lord Keynes made the orthodox economist realize the need to scrutinize anew the very foundations of his subject. No serious student will ever speak again about the "simple system of natural liberty" with that graceful ease of conviction which was at least one of the grounds for the immense hold Adam Smith secured upon the thoughts of men.

Trade unions are certainly of far greater importance in

1949 than they were deemed likely to be in 1914. The membership is far greater. Their place in the life of the community is far more important. Both government and business may, in some national states, continue to be deeply hostile to them; neither, notwithstanding, can afford to ignore them. Even the legal doctrines which the long-established habits of an individualist society enabled judges to invoke against them, alike in the countries of the Common Law and of the civil law, have been changed by statutes after political struggles, the significance of which is likely to become more, and not less, apparent in the next age. It is no exaggeration to say that the status of trade unions is today far higher, and their power far greater, than it was a generation ago. No doubt they have lost some of the functions they used to perform, or, at least, some of these have become far less central to their activities than used to be the case; but they have also taken on new functions, which, as one examines them, involve immensely greater social responsibilities than before 1914. It is noteworthy, I think, that in 1914 only one trade unionist had ever sat in the British cabinet. By 1945 their presence in the cabinet had become a normal feature of the political landscape, and the evidence is unmistakable that success in war depended upon the power of the government concerned to secure the effective cooperation of the trade unions. Nor is it less obvious that the growth of complexity in the relationships inside the modern community has made the trade unions in the essential services—coal, power, and transport are simple examples—more pivotal than they have been in any previous period.

It is not fanciful on my part to argue that, of all organizations in a community like the United States or Great Britain, the character and purpose of the trade union are most elusive. One school of American social thought, the center of which has been the remarkable group of observers at the University of Wisconsin, has argued that the primary purpose of the trade union has been job-control; and it has regarded the assumption of any other purposes as either an error of judgment ultimately bound to fail, or as a misreading of what is possible in the social environment of the United States. Most of us in Great Britain, especially since 1918, are convinced that the trade unions form the most valuable center around which an effective socialist party can be built; and since we believe that, in essence, history has lessened the gap between the Conservative party and the Liberal party, we think the trade unions which confined their primary purpose to job-control would, sooner or later, present the businessmen and the politicians of the United States with insoluble problems, within the framework of a capitalist society, so long as the unions continued to grow in numbers and in power. Our experience in Great Britain since 1918 has had comparatively little influence on the formal habits and announced purposes of trade unions in France and in Italy. They still remain in both these countries structurally distinct from socialist parties, even though there has been a tendency for trade unionists, not as trade unionists but as citizens, to think with the Left and to vote with the Left. The situation is complicated in Europe—it is even complicated in the United States—by the fact that in almost every country men and women of communist views have sought, with immense energy, and not seldom with remarkable success, to permeate trade unions and to make them, as far as they could, the instruments of purposes which, in the last analysis, look to revolutionary overthrow of the present social order. Not since the emerging capitalist order gave birth to the trade unions, around the beginning of the nineteenth century, has anything influenced their habits of mind

as profoundly as the Russian Revolution and the successful
establishment of the Soviet state power. But it is far from
easy to estimate how, and for what purposes, it has influenced them. In 1920, under pressure of public opinion
among British trade unionists, Mr. Ernest Bevin approved
the movement in the Transport and General Workers' Union
to make impossible any further support of that effort, mainly
started by Mr. Winston Churchill, to overthrow the Bolshevik government by supporting in different ways their
opponents, such as Denikin and Kolchak and Wrangel. In
1949 Mr. Ernest Bevin, as the Foreign Secretary in the first
Labour government with a majority in Great Britain, not
only stands in the forefront of the opposition to what he believes to be a determined effort at communist expansionism
led by the Russian government; but no influence is greater
than his in the effort to persuade the British trade unions to
prevent the Communists among their members from acquir-
ing positions which might enable them to throw the influence of the unions to the side supporting Soviet Russia.
Yet, without the political relationship between the Socialist
party and trade unions formally free of a political affiliation,
French and Italian trade unions are the major source of communist strength in their respective countries. History, beyond mistake, is the breeding ground of paradoxes which
seem born to confuse the analyst.

Much of the judgment we make about the role the trade
unions are to play in the modern state is likely to depend
upon our philosophy of the state in the kind of national
community we know in Western civilization. If we accept
the philosophy of Soviet Russia, the trade unions cease to be
organs independent of the government and become, however important, only one of the instruments through which
those who dominate the government are able to carry out

their purposes. They are committed; especial functions are allotted to them. The major figures in their organization are clearly significant in the life of the Russian community. But they are not organs empowered to do more than make representation to the Council of People's Ministers and other bodies; they have lost any voluntary character they once possessed; above all, they have lost the right to strike. The places of pivotal importance in their directorate, at almost every level of their operation, are in the hands of members of the Communist party, so that, in a general way, the contours of the policy ultimately worked out are determined by an authority which, though closely related to the unions, does not spring directly from it and can hardly be described as directly responsible to it. The character of the unions, in a word, is set by the fact that they function in a one-party state in which, for the normal purposes of practical life, state and party are one. The party representatives in the unions are therefore, in effect, almost as much representatives of the government of Soviet Russia as if they sat in the legislature; and, subject to their receptivity to the criticism of the proposals they place before trade-union organizations, they are convinced that their principles will prevail. For once they have secured acceptance of those principles, it follows logically from the inherent nature of the one-party state that organized opposition to the trade-union leadership is organized opposition to the only permissible party. Since this party is the state, organized opposition in the trade union becomes something it is difficult not to describe as conspiracy against the state. The scope of trade-union strategy is not, therefore, set by the opinions and sentiments of the members; it is set by the limits of what the state authority, through its approved organ, is prepared to accept as desirable.

It may well be said, in criticism of this view, that the Russian situation is special in that, first, it is the outcome of a socialist revolution, in which history has rendered it still necessary to maintain the dictatorship of the proletariat over the workers through the agency of the party as their vanguard; when the socialist revolution has, internally and externally, reached an unassailable position, the workers can expect relief from the subordination to the party, which is now the real master of their habits. To this is added, in part with considerable truth, that the trade-union membership welcomes much of the criticism it calls "constructive": criticism, that is to say, which they are assured comes from a spirit of goodwill toward, and not from hostility to, the regime. Certainly at the lower level of relations between trade-union members and management over problems which touch matters like output, technique or production, absenteeism, the adaptation of machinery that the workers' "know how" will continually suggest, the problems of vocational training, and cultural opportunities, there can be no reasonable doubt that, granted the assurance of goodwill, criticism is genuinely welcome and seriously considered; more, that it will be put to the factory director or his assistants with all the cogency that the trade unions can muster. I add that, as far as my own observation extends, the managerial side of industry will give far greater attention to representations of this kind than is generally the case in the United States of America or Great Britain or France, especially where technological improvement is concerned. If it be said that, nevertheless, the technical competence of a Russian factory is at a far lower level, generally speaking, than in the advanced countries of the West, and that, despite the formal principles of Soviet law, safeguards in the mines, for instance, against loss of life or injury are a good deal less adequate than they are in the United States or Great Britain, I should be inclined to agree. But I think it is wholly reasonable to urge in reply that Russia has sought to make a population overwhelmingly peasant in character recognize in one generation habits that elsewhere have been painfully acquired in over a century of disciplined experience. Forcible and speedy adaptation is a Russian habit of long standing, for which the rulers of contemporary Russia have far less responsibility than their predecessors. It is Russian, too, to value the safety of life and limb at a lower rate than it is general to expect in the West. I should add, further, that a generalization as wide as this is subject to important exceptions, like the long years in the West in which there was a shocking failure to pay proper attention to the prevention and cure of industrial diseases, such as miners' nystagmus or silicosis. And I should certainly feel confident that the attention given by the Soviet trade unions to the post-entry training of their members, vocational and cultural alike, is far more profound and enthusiastic than the similar effort of trade unions in Western countries.

The other argument in defense of the Russian position must not be omitted. In a society largely capitalist, it is said, the inherent antagonism between the employers and the workers makes the function of the trade unions above everything defensive in character. The trade unions defend the workers' standard of life, especially in periods of depression, against attacks which come from every quarter. Where unemployment is the whip which enforces discipline, and where the employers' search for profit is the central motive of the economic system, it is wholly natural that the trade unions should maximize their independence of the state power since the operation of the state power is, by its very nature, bound to be on the side of the employers. The area in which the government of a capitalist country can be neutral, it is said, still more the area in which it can be favorable to the workers, is necessarily small. Both the law and the administration of a capitalist society are directed essentially to the support of the employers; it is therefore natural for the unions to insist upon their right to as fully independent a judgment as they can make, because, normally, the scales are weighted against the interest of the workers. In a socialist society, on the other hand, this basic antagonism is removed. Workers and managers share in a common purpose which gives unity to the whole society. The trade unions are then not merely defensive; they also have the obligation to assist, by all means in their power, in fulfilling the objectives at which the government aims in its plan. There is no inherent divergence of interest between the objectives of the trade union and those of the government, because, as the latter are realized, the members of the trade unions, in their capacity as citizens, share in each additional "dose" of well-being made possible by the increase of output. The trade unions in Soviet Russia have become, in a sense with which capitalist societies cannot be acquainted, a consultative instrument for carrying out governmental purposes of which they are themselves the beneficiaries. Were they to slow down unjustifiably the rate of work, or, further, were they to go on strike, they would be inflicting injury upon themselves and not upon a class which has an interest antagonistic to their own.

It cannot be denied that, in abstraction, there is a real truth in this view for anyone who accepts Marxism as it has been modified by Lenin, and, still more, by Stalin. But, equally, it cannot be denied that the process of abstraction is important or that the defense of this attitude depends upon one's view of the validity of Stalinism. The abstraction

is based upon the assumptions that the government is aiming
at the welfare of the common people, and also that its
interpretation of that welfare is indisputable. There is thus
no way open to workers as citizens to change the character
of their government by the expression of their view at free
elections. The validity of Stalinism, in its turn, is based upon
the assumption that, in a broad way, present consumption
must be regarded as secondary to arrival at that stage of
economic development where general abundance has replaced general scarcity. It is, for instance, clear that the acceptance of the principle of socialism in a single country
means a Russia surrounded, in its government's eyes, by
capitalist states anxious for its destruction. This involves an
exceptionally large military budget; Soviet Russia not only
spends a larger proportion of its national income upon defense than any other country in the world, but holds under
arms a larger standing army than the total force of all other
European states, if we omit the armies of the countries allied
to it in Eastern Europe. This means about five million men
withdrawn from productive industry. It means also that
those engaged in the manufacture of the necessary equipment for the armed forces are withdrawn from the provision
of capital goods and services, as well as consumers' goods
and services, which would do much to advance the time
when the era of scarcity would give way to the era of abundance. It is important to remember that this is an area of
policy-making with which the trade unions have no concern
at all. Nor have they any direct say, either, in deciding the
scale upon which the well-being of the present generation
is to be postponed in the interest of a posterity which may
hope to enjoy abundance. A Moscow worker and his family,
sharing a room with several other families in a ramshackle
and obsolete tenement house, may possibly lack the inner

conviction which persuades him that the government is right in delaying the satisfaction of his desire for an apartment of his own to its judgment of Russian military needs today or of its plans for a spacious and well-planned Moscow he will not live to see. He may well approve with passionate intensity these decisions of the government. The point I am concerned to make is that it is not really open to him through his trade union (or indeed through any other organization) to make his opinion so explicit that the government must take account of it. The relation of the trade union to the state in Soviet Russia means that in matters of this kind the worker is handed decisions he is unable to affect unless he is a Communist party official of importance. That achievement of eminence apart, his way out lies through his ability to become a Stakhanovite of outstanding skill, or to enter an occupation which is so esteemed by the government that its members are able, so to speak, to enjoy in the present the material well-being which the future will lay open to all. But, if he be the ordinary worker, his well-being is not attained through any influence his trade union can exert upon his behalf, still less at his instigation.

In the non-socialist and highly industrialized states of the West the trade unions have played a role the character of which is largely independent of their governments, save in those cases where, as in Italy under Mussolini, or Germany under Hitler, their normal functions have been suspended. We must, indeed, be careful not to exaggerate their independence of their governments. Any scrutiny of the normal position will reveal a variety of limitations upon their independence, the significance of which may be profound. Practically every government possesses powers, akin to those at the disposal of the British government under the Emergency Powers Act of 1920, that would enable it, in any critical situation, to protect the "community" by making provision, under penalty, for the continuity of vital services. Labor governments in Europe have, on more than one occasion, invoked these powers against trade unions on strike in essential industries. The action of M. Briand, in breaking the French railway strike of 1910 by calling up all the relevant strikers involved to their army service, in order to safeguard the "community," is illustrative of this point. It is important that, in 1948, when American coal mines were under the President's control, an injunction was granted against the miners' union on the ground that it could not strike in an industry under government control, and that the miners' union and Mr. John L. Lewis as well were held in contempt of court and fined for refusing to call off the strike. Not less interesting is the claim made by President Truman, at his press conference of February 4, 1949, that there was inherent in his office the constitutional power to prohibit strikes that affect the national health or welfare; nor must we overlook the fact that the bill to repeal the Taft-Hartley Act contains a clause which calls for a postponement of any strike for thirty days—in the hope that a settlement may be reached during this period—whenever the President has ruled that the potential strike may affect vital national interests. I presume that similar powers might be exercised if, instead of a strike, the managers or owners in a vital industry threatened a lockout with the same potential effect. I do not, however, know of any case in which this immense authority has been used against the employers. Certainly no such power was invoked by Benjamin Harrison in the Homestead lockout of 1892, which lasted nearly five months; nor was it invoked against the Pullman Company in 1894, when in the race to make the dispute a lockout rather than a strike —a race which the company just lost—the directors of the

Pullman Company announced that their plants would be closed indefinitely and actually kept them closed for just on three months. The Pullman affair is exceptionally illuminating since the American Railway Union and its leader, Eugene Debs, exhausted every possible means to secure a settlement by negotiation. When this was refused, not only did the other railroads, through the General Managers' Association, come at once to the assistance of the Pullman Company, but, by a remarkable intrigue and over the protests of both Mayor Hopkins of Chicago and Governor Altgeld of Illinois, they persuaded the federal government, first, to swear in thousands of deputy sheriffs, who were, in fact, strikebreakers; second, to use federal troops in their support; and third, through the agency of Richard Olney, the Attorney-General in President Cleveland's cabinet, to secure an injunction against the union as guilty of malicious conspiracy against twenty-three railroads. For a refusal to obey this injunction Eugene Debs was held in contempt and sentenced to six months' imprisonment, and three of his colleagues to three months' imprisonment in each case. It is a sidelight of some interest that, when the strike had been broken, the Pullman Company, though strongly condemned for its attitude to the American Railway Union by the Senate committee of inquiry, nevertheless did not even trouble to answer a letter from Governor Altgeld asking it to forego rent arrears and to charge no rent for about a month to the strikers and their families, though they were on the verge of starvation. Altgeld had to aid them as best he could through the medium of a public distress fund.

I do not cite the Pullman strike as an example of the habits of the judiciary in relation to the trade unions; I reserve that for later discussion. I am anxious to make one vital principle clear: that even in political communities where the trade unions are independent of the state power, where most of industry and agriculture are in private hands critical conditions compel the modern government, if it thinks important aspects of the national life are threatened —in the mining industry, for example, or in transport—to transform an independent movement into one which must obey the state power. The government has always the decisive word in a dispute. I want to emphasize this for a number of reasons. First, it is a theory of the state because it assumes that the government of a community is sovereign; it gives orders to all other societies in the community, if it wishes to do so, and receives orders from none of them. This is, of course, a formal juristic frame of reference. It is part of the theory that all voluntary bodies are subordinate to the government whenever the latter wishes to insist on subordination. The ground for this claim appears to be that no other organization in the community but the government can assure to it the continuance of those vital services upon which a life as complex and interdependent as that of a highly industrialized community necessarily depends. It is a power, in theory, to be exercised without regard to the issue of where right and wrong lie in the actual dispute. When the continuance of the service is assured, the government may or may not decide to intervene, either to see that right prevails, or, by methods of conciliation, to secure a settlement which the parties to the dispute are willing to accept. In part, obviously, once continuity of service is assured, the government reverts either to the position of a disinterested spectator keeping the ring, or to that of an arbitrator who hears an argument and makes a decision, or, again, to that of a friendly mediator using the prestige attached to its function to effect some kind of compromise. What we have to realize is how rare it is for a government to arbitrate and impose a view it believes to be just. President Wilson did that during the First World War when, in view of the impending conflict on the railroads, he persuaded Congress, in 1916, to pass the Adamson Law. Thereby, broadly speaking, he gave the railroad brotherhoods what they were seeking on the ground that their claim was justified. A decision of this character by the government is uncommon; and it is permissible to doubt whether President Wilson would have made it if he had not been faced with a critical emergency situation; it is certainly still more doubtful whether, but for that emergency, the Supreme Court of the United States would have then held the Adamson Law to be constitutional.

But we must pursue this analysis still further. Whether a government prevents conflict in a vital industry by simple prohibition of any interruption of the service, or by insisting upon a "cooling off" period while means of a settlement are sought, the important thing for us to notice is that the unions concerned are denied the right to strike. Now, since the right to strike is perhaps the most important ultimate weapon a trade union possesses, its denial, in all cases of this kind, throws a very clear light upon the government as a neutral element in industrial disputes. There was no such attack, until the Wagner Act of 1935, on the vital weapons of the employers—the use of the lockout, the refusal to deal with genuine trade unions, and the denial of the view that all workers may be driven to accept the yellow-dog contract.

This is really to say that, outside the area of interstate commerce, as defined in the Wagner Act, the employer is able, in industrial disputes in a vital industry, to use the state power as a weapon against the union.

With the Wagner Act, which conferred upon the National Labor Relations Board the right, through the Circuit Court of Appeals, to secure the approval of the judiciary for its purposes, there was a vital change.

From 1935 to 1946, when the Taft-Hartley Act amended the Wagner Act almost to a point where it was unrecognizable, it really seemed as though the unions might hope to fight the employers on pretty equal terms. On this basis, the government was seeking to disembarrass itself from the complex task of choosing between the rights and wrongs of all parties to a dispute. It did this by saying, in the Norris-La Guardia Act, that it prohibited the use of injunction in labor disputes, and, in the Wagner Act, that the employer must negotiate with the organization his employees have freely chosen to act on their behalf.

"The labor movement," said Mr. Justice Jackson in his dissent in the Hunt case, "has come full circle. The workingman has struggled long, the fight has been filled with hatred, and the conflict has been dangerous, but now workers may not be deprived of their livelihood merely because their employers oppose and they favor unions. Labor has won other rights as well, unemployment compensation, old age benefits, and, what is most important and the basis of all its gains, the recognition that the opportunity to earn his support is not alone the concern of the individual, but is the problem with which all organized societies must contend and conquer, if they are to survive. This Court now sustains the claim of a union to the right to deny participation in the economic world to an employer simply because the union dislikes him. This Court permits to employees the same arbitrary dominance over the economic sphere which they control, which labor so long, so bitterly, and so rightly asserted should belong to no man."

My concern here is not merely to point out that where a

government takes the view that a crisis is imminent in a vital
industry it reduces the relevant trade unions to a position of
dependence upon its will. My point is, further, that, so far
as I am aware, that view is not taken when the initiative to
reasonable settlement rests with the employers' side.

That emerged very strikingly in the steel strike of 1919
in the United States and in the coal strike of 1926 in Great
Britain. In the first case, the intention of President Wilson
to impose the eight-hour day upon the steel industry was
frustrated by the end of the war; but it is significant that the
steel corporation and the unions were left to fight it out, as
though the government were in duty bound to be neutral
once the national crisis had passed. Yet all serious observers
of the steel industry condemned with vigor the harsh intrac-
tability of Judge Gary and his associates and denounced the
indefensibly long hours they imposed upon the steel workers.

What explains the neutrality of the government toward
employers who, in an important industry like steel, force
upon their men conditions which are the result of the corporation's superior power, without regard to any principles
of justice or of social welfare?

Almost the same issue arose in the British coal strike of
1926. The main factor leading to the strike—in which the
issues were wages and hours of labor—was the decision of
the British government to return to the gold standard with
the pound at its prewar value in terms of dollars. That this
was an ill-judged decision I have no need to demonstrate,
since the late Lord Keynes has shown it to be so in one of
the most brilliant pamphlets [1] he ever wrote. Among the results of the decision was the need to reduce the price of
British coal for export, which the employers proposed to do

[1] John Maynard Keynes, *The Economic Consequences of Mr. Churchill*
(London: L. & V. Woolf, 1925).

by lengthening hours and reducing wages. For some months conflict between the mine owners and the miners was postponed, while a commission of inquiry, under the chairmanship of Sir Herbert (now Viscount) Samuel, investigated the situation. By their terms of reference, they could not deal with anything outside the superficial causes of the dispute; in particular, they could not say that any wise government returning to the gold standard would have recommended the devaluation of the pound in terms of the dollar. Accepting the necessity for Great Britain to export coal, and knowing that the government would not continue its subsidy to the industry beyond May 1, 1926, the Samuel Commission had no alternative but to recommend a reduction in wages. Since these were already low, and made even lower by the fact that thousands of mines were not on full time, the miners decided to strike. It will be remembered that their position awakened such sympathy among the other unions in the Trades Union Congress that its General Council decided upon a national strike in sympathy with them. While negotiations with the government were proceeding in the hope of preventing this catastrophe, the printers on the *Daily Mail* —not, I think, the most responsible of English newspapers— refused to set up an editorial which they believed to be grossly unfair and fantastically inaccurate.

The government at once used this action as a pretext for breaking off all negotiations with the unions. The general strike occurred—let me add, a strike notable for its discipline, the absence of disorder, and the refusal of its leaders to allow it to become more than a great gesture of goodwill to the miners—and the government at once took up the position that they could not consider negotiation, since they confronted a threat unconstitutionally to coerce the government to act in a way for which it was not prepared. In ten days

the General Council abjectly surrendered. I refrain from
analyzing the complete causes of this. But the miners, with
remarkable courage, fought on for almost six months and
submitted to the owners' demands only because they and
their families were literally starved into defeat. I doubt
whether the full tale of victimization and suffering they
underwent from 1926 to the outbreak of war in 1939 will
ever be told in anything like its true tragic proportions. I
content myself with the remark that if the victors at the
general election of 1945 had not, as soon as they became a
government, announced their intention to transfer the mines
to national ownership, they would have been faced in every
mining area with a strike in which the bitterness of the
miners would have made it impossible to avoid violence, and
perhaps bloodshed. And it must be remembered that thousands of those who went back to the mining areas were the
trained and resolute veterans of the Second World War who
could not have been persuaded to undergo the humiliation
and the suffering of the interwar years a second time.

The significance of this British illustration is twofold. In
the first place it brings out very clearly the way in which
the juristic conception of the state as sovereign gives to the
government of the day a special political, and even psychological, status in relation to trade unions. This status makes
the latter deal with the government upon the assumption
that they are subordinate associations. In the second place it
makes it obvious that the major emphasis of governmental
service in an industrial dispute is bound to be to the disadvantage of labor.

In the strike of 1926 the miners were the victims of the
combined and determined pressure of the Treasury and the
Bank of England upon Mr. Churchill, then Chancellor of
the Exchequer, to return to the gold standard on terms nec-

essarily detrimental to all British exports and therefore to coal. When this became clear, there is no evidence that the government thought of devaluation as the proper remedy; what it did was to subsidize the mining industry until it had completed preparations which made the defeat of the miners inevitable.

It is illuminating to compare that determination to stay on the gold standard in 1926, as a principle necessary to British economic salvation, with the readiness of the "National" government in 1931 to go off the gold standard, even though less than a fortnight before Mr. Ramsay MacDonald had formed his "National" government on the basis that at all costs the gold standard must be preserved. I draw from this the inference that the occasions are exceptionally rare when the government, even if its composition is progressive, is able to use the state power it operates on behalf of the trade unions, except in a special crisis like that of war. Even then such use is exceptional.

Mr. Churchill became Prime Minister in 1940, after the disasters in Norway, very largely because the Labour party would serve under no other leader at a moment when it was imperative to have a government of national unity. But it is notable that throughout his five years of office he refused to be responsible for what he called "controversial" legislation and that he interpreted "controversial" legislation to be any proposed statute unpalatable to his Conservative supporters. The very important result of this attitude was that when victory came in Europe in the spring of 1945 no serious preparations had been made for peace. We were, as we all knew, entering a new and difficult world; Mr. Churchill himself has described some of its difficulties in a well-known conversation with Mr. Henry Morgenthau, then the American Secretary of the Treasury. By refusing to attempt the adjust-

ment of Great Britain and its government to the needs of
that new world, Mr. Churchill was, quite consciously, refusing to organize the dynamic it was urgent to have ready in
anticipation of the great demands he himself already knew
would be made upon the minds and energies of a people
fatigued by nearly six years of intense fighting.

I conclude from all this that whether trade unions, as in
Russia, are simply a specialized agency of the government,
or whether, as in Great Britain or the United States, they
are voluntary associations which settle their union policy in
their own way, crisis in either type of community makes
trade unions dependent upon the government. They are
compelled to subordinate their desires to its commands.
Their alternative is the obvious one of attempting a revolution, in which, if it is successful, they overthrow the government and, taking its place, set up their own organization to
operate the state power.

I conclude, moreover, that in a capitalist society where an
industrial dispute is held to affect the community in a serious
way, the incidence of the intervention which any government attempts will normally—the case of war being an exception—be to the advantage of an owning class and its
managerial agents, and to the disadvantage of trade unionism.

That is so even where, as in Great Britain, a Labour government is in power but faces a position in which the sector of
publicly owned and operated industry is small and the main
character of ownership is capitalist. In such a case, while the
Labour government is the bearer of state power in a formal
sense, factually the authority concentrated in private ownership and control sets drastic limits to the area within which
that state power may be used. The same is true in France,
where the Socialist party cooperates in a coalition govern-

ment. That government cannot yield, in the mining industry, to the demands of the miners, even though it knows that most of them are just; at the same time it cannot collect the full measure of taxes due either from the mass of peasants or from a number of citizens of great wealth among the *haute bourgeoisie* and from great corporations without risk to its authority. I do not for one moment suggest that if all Frenchmen had a sufficiently deep civic spirit to pay their taxes willingly (remember Mr. Justice Holmes' remark to his secretary that he paid his taxes willingly because, with them, he bought civilization) the government of France would be able to meet the miners' claims; but I do suggest that some part of the anger felt when the demands are refused would disappear because there would be a greater faith than there now is in the just incidence of the government's power. As it is, the French government suffers, as the British government suffers, from the fact that, however real its goodwill, the capitalist nature of the community over which it rules handicaps any effort it may make to give equal treatment to all its citizens, whether they belong to the employing class or to the class the power of which is so largely determined by the strength of its trade unions.

2

Since the end of the First World War, as I have said, the status of the trade unions almost everywhere has been changing, usually for the better. There are, of course, variations in the dynamic of the change. Where there has been successful counterrevolution, as, notably, under Mussolini and Hitler and Franco, the change of status has been for the worse. In the United States there has been a notable upward swing since 1933, in Great Britain since 1919, in France, the five years of German occupation apart, since the grave threat of February 1934, in Italy, in the North, since the overthrow of Mussolini in 1943. The change is marked in a number of ways. In part, it is shown by the fact that functions hitherto undertaken by the trade unions for their members only are accepted by governments and applied to all citizens to whom they are relevant; it is, for example, extraordinarily illuminating to compare the attitude in the United States toward unemployment insurance in the 1920's with the attitude in the 1940's. A second criterion is the importance attached to the trade-union vote.

In different political systems, of course, that importance is expressed in a different way. Note, for example, the contrast between the attitude of negligent indifference shown toward the unions by both parties in 1896, with the recognition of Mr. Sidney Hillman's pivotal importance in the presidential campaigns of 1936 to 1944; and it is said, on good authority, that one of the first acts of President Truman, after his victory in 1948, was to thank Mr. Philip Murray for the trade-union support he had received in that contest.

The same mood, of course, exists in British politics. I doubt whether any person other than Ernest Bevin could have secured the eager cooperation of the trade unions in the wartime labor legislation Mr. Churchill's government deemed it necessary to impose; and Mr. Attlee's government would not last a week if the support of the Trades Union Congress were withdrawn from it. The change in status is marked both by the content of legislation and by the care now taken by most governments to associate the trade unions with the consultations which generally precede its introduction into the legislative assembly.

I do not venture to guess what part the association of the Republican party with the Taft-Hartley Act played in the defeat of Governor Dewey; but I suspect that it was at least as intimate as the part played by the Trade Union Law Amendment Act of 1927 in securing the defeat of Mr. Baldwin and the Conservative party in Great Britain in 1929.

There is another criterion of importance. Until this last generation the ability of the trade union to attract to its ranks what Americans call the "white-collar" and Englishmen the "black-coated" workers was small. Today it is steadily increasing; and though it would be an exaggeration to say that the manual workers' doubts of the "white-collar" workers have gone, the old suspicions are beginning to disappear, and the signs point to steadily greater alliance between them. The Newspaper Guild, like the American Federation of Teachers, has had a history which, in the steady succession of booms and slumps, somewhat resembles the evolution of capitalism; nevertheless, both of them have come to stay, and both of them are likely to play an increasingly important part in the development of social legislation.

Of the non-manual trade unions in Great Britain affiliated to the Trades Union Congress, I should like especially to draw your attention to the Association of Scientific Workers. It is attracting to its ranks the bulk of the younger scientists and technicians in industry, and many of the younger men who specialize in pure science are joining because they are recognizing, more and more each year, that all science has a social interest. The place of science in our social life suffers greatly when scientists seek to retreat to the ivory tower and pray for a detachment from the actual life outside. For that actual life comes nearer each day to the entrance they once hoped would pass unnoticed.

It is something more than accident that the half-dozen outstanding specialists in the Second World War were all trade unionists in good standing; one of them, Professor

P. M. S. Blackett, has within this last year been awarded the
Nobel Prize in Physics. I venture the prophecy that ten years
from now this aspect of the trade-union movement will have
a far greater importance than it has today. I believe that
scientists everywhere are more aware of their civilizations
than at any time since the seventeenth century. Anyone who
reads Thomas Sprat's classic *History of the Royal Society*,
first published in 1667, will note his remark that the Society
was to find a doctrine "for the use of cities, and not for the
retirement of schools." The Society, indeed, was to resemble
the city, in that it was to be composed of all sorts and conditions of men. It was to have no barriers between classes.
"By bringing philosophy down again to men's sight and
practice, whence it has flown away so high, the Royal Society has put it into a position of standing out against the
invasions of time, or even barbarism itself." The Royal
Society, at least for the first generation of its history, did
genuinely set out to discover knowledge "for the benefit and
relief of the state and the society of man," to use those
famous words Bacon had written some fifty years before.

I do not believe men of science have felt this duty as intimately as now for nearly three centuries; and I believe it to
be of high importance that they look for support in their
effort more and more to the trade unions. In the degree that
they make the unions science-conscious, in the fullest sense
of that term, I think they put behind their purpose the one
major element in society most likely, and most able, to free
them from servitude to secretive governments on the one
hand, and from dependence upon interests which regard
both science and technology as investments from which
profit may be extracted on the other.

Looking at the situation in France and Great Britain,

above all in its contemporary perspective, it seems to me possible that the partnership between the man of science and the trade unionist may be one of the surest ways we have to protect freedom of research from bureaucratic domination, and through that protection to place the benefit of scientific discovery at the disposal of mankind.

This alliance opens up other vistas down which we must briefly gaze. I hardly need to emphasize here the complex nature of trade unionism or the thick fog of prejudice, both friendly and hostile, in which its serious study has been obscured. It is, of course, not merely an economic problem, the problem of the way in which the worker in any union can use his bargaining power, in company with his fellow members, to get the best possible conditions for himself in his contract with his employer. It is not merely economic either, because it is so closely related to methods of production, whether that involve the use of machinery, the speed of work, the training of apprentices, the costs of distribution, or the place of scientific management in the search for efficiency. All these economic aspects, and many more, are no doubt of outstanding importance; but, taken alone, they no more enable us to understand trade unionism than we can do if we argue, like the late Professor Henry Simons of Chicago, that it is the worst and most ugly of monopolies, or, like some of the anti-union propaganda of the National Association of Manufacturers, that it is the work of evil-minded agitators seeking to destroy what, without them, would be readily perceived to be a natural harmony of interests between employers and their workmen. Nor will it be understood if we regard it, on the one hand, as the obvious way in which specialized groups of workers seek to protect their peculiar interests against newcomers to a particular trade, or, on the other, as the most direct road so far dis-covered along which the workers can march to the achieve-ment of man's highest hopes and dreams.

The study of trade unionism, especially in recent years, has a multiformity of possible analysis which makes it touch all the social sciences at some point. Sometimes it touches one of them more closely than another; that depends very largely upon the questions we ask about it, and the meaning of the questions, and, still more, of the answers that the facts on analysis reveal.

Perhaps it is still necessary to emphasize, as did the late Professor Hoxie—after Sidney and Beatrice Webb, by all odds the profoundest student of the movement—that what he called the "union problem" is, in his own words, "neither simple nor unitary. . . . On the contrary, it is a complex of economic, legal, ethical, and social problems, which can be understood and met only by knowing the facts and the genesis of the viewpoint of organized labor in all its riches, diversity, contradictions, and shifting character, and by con-sidering this viewpoint in relation to developing social con-ditions and social standards." [2] Professor Hoxie wrote those words well over a generation ago, but they are even more true today than when he wrote them. Nothing is more clear in our time than that trade unions today are pluralist in character and pragmatic in method; if they are not, they are unlikely to survive the demands made upon them by so swiftly changing an environment. Trade-union philosophy, indeed, is generally more likely to develop after the trade union has twisted and turned to adapt itself to a developing situation than while the situation, in all its rich variety, is trying to find some stable basis of equilibrium in society.

[2] Robert F. Hoxie, *Trade Unionism in the United States* (New York: Appleton, 1917), p. 36.

From the immense mass of possible aspects, I propose, therefore, to choose here only one for annotation. I want to inquire what kind of impact the Russian Revolution and the world-wide communist doctrine it has sponsored have created in trade unions, which, at least on one side of their work, have been deeply concerned to assist in building a nobler and more elevated society than any we have so far known.

I do not believe there is a single answer to this question. But I do believe that the issues it raises are of far-reaching importance and are likely to be more, and not less, important in the next twenty-five years. Nothing has done so much as the impact of Soviet Russia to demonstrate among trade unions everywhere the conviction that mass unemployment is not a necessary element in economic organization. Nothing has done so much, either, to destroy all over the world any serious faith in laissez faire. If we go behind the words to the realities they seek to describe, I think it is probable that many American trade unionists, at least trade unionists of high eminence in both branches of the American labor movement, would find themselves far stronger advocates of democratic socialist planning than they believe themselves to be. When an eminent union official, for example, tells an English newspaper "that he sees no reason for objecting to a capitalist system so long as it continually increases wages, is not monopolistic, and does not make excessive profits," adding that "he favored legislation to enforce competition if it began to be transformed into monopoly," [3] I think, with great regret, that he was asking that a capitalist system should not act in a capitalist way. There is no evidence that this is likely to happen, in the United States or anywhere else. What he is really seeking is a capitalism that safeguards the

[3] *Evening Standard* (London), Feb. 7, 1949.

workers against unemployment, uses all its energies to make
statutes like the Sherman Act really work, and is free from
those predatory features of which Thorstein Veblen wrote
so brilliantly.

I well understand such an approach. Its exponent feels
that a highly successful capitalism will, save for housing,
which he notes as an exceptional case requiring government
assistance, enable trade unions mainly to confine their activities to job-control; they will thus be enabled to avoid that
growing immersion in large political problems which gives
members of the Communist party their opportunity to exercise their zealous activity in trade unions. Not least, it will
enable the trade unions to evade the very difficult problem
of whether they can continue to act through existing political parties and avoid, as the British Trades Union Congress
avoided until 1899, playing their special role in organizing a
new political party for which they provide the leadership.

I recognize, too, that this trade-union official spoke in the
aftermath of Mr. Truman's remarkable victory, toward
which American labor made so considerable a contribution,
and during the course of which President Truman pledged
himself to the repeal of the Taft-Hartley Act.

I recognize further that he was speaking almost immediately after the withdrawal of the CIO and the Trades
Union Congress from the World Federation of Trade Unions,
on the ground that the World Federation was, above all, a
superb platform for that communist propaganda to which
trade-union officials, and the CIO and the Trades Union
Congress generally, are stoutly opposed.

I submit, very respectfully, that the facts have already
long outdistanced this approach. This view of what capitalism might be has never been true, and there is no evidence,
even in the United States, that it is likely to be in our time.

If those who think in this way would consider the evidence submitted to the Temporary National Economic Committee in 1938, and realize that the problems it advanced are only obscured for a period by the special postwar conditions, I think they would see why President Roosevelt, on April 29, 1938, in his message to Congress requesting an inquiry into the concentration of economic power, could say that "the liberty of a democracy is not safe if the people tolerate the growth of private power to a point where it becomes stronger than their democratic state itself. . . . Concentration of economic power and the resulting unemployment of labor and capital are inseparable problems for a modern 'private enterprise' democracy." To this I would add the conclusion reached in 1942 by Senator James E. Murray, as chairman of the Senate Committee on Small Business. "Small business for many years," he said, "has been waging a losing fight against its big competitors. The growing concentration of economic control and the extension of monopolistic practices has become appalling." [4] To these observations I must add the fact that all the evidence confirms the belief that the war has accelerated this concentration and monopoly even more rapidly than in the interwar years. Anyone, moreover, who considers the very limited recommendations the Temporary National Economic Committee felt it was able to make will realize that these involve action, mostly of a legislative character, which goes down to the very roots of the American economy. They touch very closely immensely powerful private interests, both federal and state, which have profound influence over the executive and legislative powers directly, and, naturally, the judicial power also. In the light of the facts I do not think I am being unfair to a practical

[4] Hearings before the U.S. Senate Committee on Small Business, 76th Cong., 1st sess., Part I, p. 2.

official's attitude, however eminent he be, if I say that it belongs to the era of capitalism before the Civil War and that this conception of trade-union functions is fixed by the kind of business unionism of which the American Federation of Labor was sponsor under the leadership of Samuel Gompers. The rapidly changing conditions of American economic life have forced the workers to reach out far beyond the conceptions with which Mr. Gompers was satisfied. At each point of importance, moreover, where they do reach out, the workers find that they have a political problem to face, and they have to face it, save under temporary boom conditions, in the spirit of those words spoken by Franklin Roosevelt which I have just quoted.

Labor leaders agree that private enterprise in housing has failed and suggest the need of government assistance to make up for its failure. I know of no evidence in any country in the world today that proves that government assistance for low-cost housing even begins to solve the problem. The scale is too vast; the amount of subsidy required creates a demand for building materials which simply increases tomorrow the price at which a house could be built yesterday. And to that must be added the fact that public authorities which set out to assist the building industry find that the relevant industries which supply its materials are honeycombed with every sort of price-fixing device from the real-estate people who sell the land at one end, to the manufacturers who supply the fixtures of a bathroom at the other. The price-fixing devices are the outcome of the lesson private employers have learned—that there is far more profit in combination than there is in competition.

The more the housing problem under a private enterprise system is examined, the less is the capacity revealed to solve it; and it is notable that Great Britain, the economy of which balances a little uneasily on a tight-rope, has since 1945 done far more than any other country, far more, even, than the United States, by placing its main reliance for the relief of the housing shortage on public rather than private enterprise.

Nor is this less revealing than the fact that, during the interwar years, low-cost housing for rent was largely left in the hands of private builders who were subsidized by the government for every house they built in this area. Yet they proved wholly unsuccessful in their effort to overcome the problem. The same story might be told of France, as it might be told of Germany and Italy and the Scandinavian countries.

The view I am led to take by the labor-unions' approach is that political questions of real importance are involved at every stage. This makes it imperative for trade unions to have a policy, which may be empirical in its daily approach, but must, nevertheless, be informed by a body of long-term principles, by what, in fact, is a philosophy of this kind. It may be one that most of us reject; it may still fail to do much more than insist that the American unions must not follow the Moscow road. But it has the important advantage that it gives trade unionism a context in the whole of national life. You may reject, as I do, the context it provides, but it does, at least, try to think out what American trade unions ought to be doing in 1949 and not in 1889. The result is that where there is a bloc of Communists in a union they have a zeal and an energy that outstrip anything normally displayed by their critics and opponents. They have these qualities because their habits are informed by a philosophy. Theirs may well be the theory of a militant minority, which in a boom period of the economy the ordinary workers find unimpressive and unattractive. But suppose that instead of a boom period the workers face a depression, perhaps equivalent in

its intensity to that of 1929—I hope I may be permitted to
say that the militant minority will exercise an influence quite
out of proportion to its strength in numbers.

That, I believe, is what is easily forgotten. With full employment, with no obvious sign of an imminent collapse in
the seller's market, with vast government activity taking
place, as in the European Recovery Program and the military program of the United States, the average trade unionist thinks that his leaders' analysis is sterling common sense.
But suppose that the trade cycle takes a downward turn,
suppose that wages fall, that hours of labor are increased,
that the number of unemployed grows quickly—then the
rank and file will turn quite as eagerly to the analysis of the
militant minority as today they are ready to reject it. And
that revision of view will be helped by the fact that in any
large and important union the tendency of the trade-union
leader is to be more and more separated in mental outlook
from his rank and file, who suddenly wake up to the fact
that, with all his authority over them, and the loyalty they
have given him when conditions were good, he cannot do
much for them when conditions are bad. He has then to hold
his own against a body of disillusioned followers. They see in
the losses they suffer when a pay envelope is reduced, or an
injunction is used against the union, or grounds are found to
call out the police to deal with the strikers, even to call out
the militia or federal troops, the very doctrine he has urged
them to reject. When men are "set off" and become angry,
they listen to the preaching of the Communist worker and
whisper to one another that there is a great deal in what he
says. And it must not be forgotten that only too often his
point will be proved for him by the employers' associations.
There is, after all, no single objective the labor leaders urge
as desirable the prevention of which is not the substance of

the main objectives of the employers' associations. And, under modern conditions, the access of employers' associations to the public through the media of modern communication, and their power to ask the state or federal government for protection against trade unionism by coercive methods, are generally far greater than anything the organized workers can attain.

To this must be added, I think, that, at least generally speaking, employers' organizations, where they are efficient, are far more likely to have a genuine social philosophy, especially in the United States, than is likely to be found in the trade unions. On the whole, the general law of property is on the employer's side. On the whole, public opinion is inclined to accept his assurance that the law is impartial. To ignore its findings is rare. On the whole, the vocal American public tends to resent the drive to the closed shop and to admire the free worker with his individual rate, who is held to be the real source of maximum output. On the whole, long and effective propaganda has inclined the public to resent the strike weapon when it is used in an industry that, like coal and transport, is of vital importance to daily public convenience, and to argue without much hesitation that government at every level has the right to interfere on behalf of the public convenience. When government proposes an immediate return to work on conditions it regards as fair, it is assumed that it becomes the union's right and duty to accept those conditions even when they fall far short of what the trade unions demand.

I am not unduly exaggerating if I say that where this occurs the employers skillfully mobilize the strength of the government, to add to their own, in their effort to give the unions that half-loaf which is said, on good authority, to be better than none. To achieve this end successfully they seek to undermine the powers of the trade union by giving to its members what appear to the public to be substantial concessions. These usually cost them little, since they are reflected in the prices they charge to the public, and at the same time blunt the edge of labor militancy. It is too little realized that this also leaves them free from invasion of their general right to control the major sphere of politics. It gives them a profound hold upon the state power, because the government officials with whom they mostly deal are, above all, anxious to obtain a compromise that will save the public from the inconvenience of a breakdown. Their good fortune is their ability to oppose a fairly attractive theory of general principles, which avoids the public's dread of a trial by force, to the empirical and opportunist approach of the unions.

At the back of all this there lies a theory which some labor leaders accept and of which the significance is overwhelming. It is the view that in a general way there is a harmony of interest between employers and employed. It then follows that with goodwill all differences can be settled on the basis of that harmony; that disputes, and especially violent disputes, are the result of a failure to recognize the reality of that harmony.

I hardly need to point out that the doctrine of the supposed harmony of interests is, historically, a propaganda device more or less coincident in origin with the birth of classical economics and intended to protect its main postulates from the devastating attacks of its early critics. I suspect, indeed, that any labor leader would have refused to accept it in, say, the little depression of 1937. It has never proved convincing to organized labor except in times of overwhelming boom; and it is one of the first concepts to be thrown overboard as boom conditions decline and the signs of a depression begin to make themselves felt.

If, therefore, we reject the obsolete view of the harmony of interests and agree that there is a permanent conflict between employers and workers, part of which may be resolved by conciliation or arbitration and part of which can be settled only by an actual trial of strength—or, at least, a threat to make that trial—between the two parties, then, I believe, the empiricism of habit, in which most contemporary leaders put their trust, has none of the fighting power which is communicated to its votaries by a doctrine like communism. For communism seems able to supply them with what they feel is the key to a complete philosophy of politics. It gives them a sense of urgency, a vigor and devotion in action, which is evoked by "business" unionism only in moments of dramatic tension. I do not for one moment deny that Communists are difficult, often reckless, capable of what, perhaps, I may term a hidden complexity of method the ethics of which raise grave problems. But we ought not to forget that these same characteristics have been displayed by union leaders in what on examination turns out to be nothing but a selfish struggle for personal power and may be something even worse than this. I am unable to accept the finality of the view put forward by Professor Perlman, for instance, with great skill, that "the manual worker is convinced that he lives in a world of limited opportunity," that though he sees immense opportunities taken hold of by others, "he decisively discounts them as far as he himself is concerned." [5]

Nor do I accept the view that what Professor Perlman

[5] Selig Perlman, *A Theory of the Labor Movement* (New York: Macmillan, 1928), p. 260.

calls the "typical manualist" knows himself to be neither a boom taker of risks nor the possessor of a sufficiently agile mind ever to feel at home in the midst of the uncertain game of competitive business. At this point Professor Perlman uses a sentence of overwhelming importance. He argues that most workers know that the larger levels of achievement are not for them, that the world has been rendered one of scarcity by an institutional order of things which purposely reserves the best opportunities for landlords, capitalists, and other privileged groups.

With great respect for Professor Perlman, I feel bound strongly to dissent from this view. I am quite certain that, with all its blunders and mistakes, the Russian Revolution has helped to awaken from inertia, and from that helpless sense that he has no right to hope, a type of workingman who, before its influence began to pervade the world, may have accepted a status of permanent inferiority akin to what was mostly imposed upon him during the Middle Ages. But the Russian Revolution is, among many other things, the symbol of a restless dynamic, which has made millions dissatisfied with their prospects and their status. It has had something like the effect of the discovery and settlement of America in opening up new and exciting vistas in people who, until its achievement, seemed to have settled down to a dull routine beyond the boundaries of which they did not dream of going. That was the effect of the French Revolution, both in 1789 and in 1848. That was the effect, also, of the Second World War upon innumerable young men and women who found themselves suddenly confronted by new and exciting possibilities in which they found it vital to adapt themselves to a new situation the implications of which radically altered the old set of habits to which they thought themselves conditioned.

The view Professor Perlman takes is, I think, one that reveals the serious limitations of that "business" unionism of which he has himself been for many years a distinguished exponent. It is a dangerous view because it discourages the worker from relating his job to the complex of social relations in which he is involved, and because its insistence upon denying to him the reality of a wider hope conditions him to the very state of mind which what Professor Perlman calls "privileged groups" desire him to accept that the basis of their privilege may go unchallenged. It then becomes virtually what I am sure Professor Perlman would never wish it to be—a weapon of great importance for the defense of the *status quo,* in a national community like the United States.

Deeply as I dissent from the principles of communist action, I am bound to say that they do at least refuse to accept the social order to which we are accustomed as in any sense a "natural" order from which there is no escape. It is, of course, obvious that the only sense in which the present order is "natural" is that it has been shaped by the historical forces of the past. What is significant in any theory of the labor movement which rejects the premises of "business" unionism is the fact that it is an active theory which relates labor policy to the whole of the social relations in which the workers are involved, instead of a passive theory which pushes those relations to the periphery—as a rule, a remote periphery of the jobs the workers do, failing to see them as the one central matter with which they are concerned. One of the grave weaknesses of this view is that it tends to persuade the worker not to look beyond the walls of the factory in which he is engaged, thereby stunting his personality and giving him that consciousness of scarcity and, therefore, pessimism about himself which Professor Perlman attributes to him. The outcome of this is to destroy the zest for innovation, the readiness to experiment with new social forms, the unwillingness to accept the position of the underprivileged as permanent, and these are the real, the dangerous, consequences of the view so strongly emphasized by Professor Perlman and his disciples. If they are right, then most of the social philosophy which led to the New Deal was wrong; and I note with interest that Professor Perlman's book, published in 1928, before the beginning of the great depression, had no expectation of its coming or of the New Deal which followed. Whatever the New Deal failed to do, it led those who accepted the philosophy of the Coolidge era to a series of steady defeats in which the labor movement played a real though limited part.

I recognize, of course, that movements change the institutions through which they express themselves, with differences set by geography and historical tradition. I do not for one moment suggest that the pattern of the British labor movement has a special authority over other patterns founded in a different experience from what we have known in Great Britain. Yet I do think there is an important quality in that tripartite alliance between the Labour party, the trade unions, and the Cooperative Movement, represented in the National Council of Labour, which puts among its major purposes an "endeavor to secure a common policy and joint action, whether by legislation or otherwise, in all questions affecting the workers as producers, consumers, and citizens." I do not pretend that the search for a common policy is always as successful as it might be, and I know from direct personal experience that differences between the Labour party and the trade unions may often be profound; it took immense effort and a considerable period, for example, for the party to persuade the unions to agree to the principle of the "rate for the job" as between men and women in work, and to support those children's allowances the benefit of which can already be accepted as proven. But I remain convinced of two things. There is no safeguard against totalitarianism as strong as a labor party, open to all who accept its principles, and built upon the mass support of organized workers, who have most to lose by totalitarianism. Nor is there any way so sure—and it is important that we should have the assurance—of getting a very important segment of the workers directly interested in the political process, and themselves taking an active part in the business of government. If I may venture the criticism, it seems to me an important weakness in the American trade unions, first, that they get their political results by acting as a pressure group, using the methods of a pressure group, both desirable and undesirable, and, second, that in their present form so few workers get direct experience, either in local government or in central government, of shaping policy for the community as a whole. That a number of eminent officials from American trade unions have held office in the President's cabinet seems to me far less important than the fact that it has not become natural to think that trade unionists might equally hope to be Secretaries of State or of the Treasury, governors of states, senators who preside over a great committee like the Senate Committee on Foreign Relations, or congressmen who take charge of the Committee on Appropriations in the House of Representatives. I take, no doubt, dramatic examples; they could, of course, be matched from every level of American political life. The trade unions in the United States obviously exercise great influence; they do not exercise responsible political power, and they do not train their members to know how to use it. They have only, so to say, a tangential relation to the political life of the United States, and I think this is both a great loss and a great danger.

That is because, in my own view, the stoutest hook we can put in Leviathan is the twofold one of effective decentralization, both by area and by function on the one hand, and the evocation, on the plane of politics, of the individual citizen's interest and initiative on the other. I do not for one moment say that we have thus hooked our Leviathan in Great Britain; I am much mistaken if it is not found, in the next decade, that a government which has mobilized great armies who give allegiance to Whitehall and the Electricity Board will have to find the way back to the loyalty which serves with ardor the City Council of Winchester or the North West Regional Board; it has, that is to say, to learn the great truth that if battles are planned by generals, they are won by captains of companies and lieutenants of platoons. The loss and the danger I see in the American theory of the relations between government and the trade unions, compared with our own in all its imperfection, is that the American theory consciously separates trade union responsibility and civic responsibility, which British theory can claim that it is at least trying to make one.

I confess to a frank fear of what I used to call the "monistic" state; the fashionable phrase of the moment is "monolithic." Its consequence is in a high degree evil. By concentrating power in a very few hands it reduces the ordinary citizen to the position of an instrument serving one end he is decreasingly permitted to define and increasingly commanded to applaud, with the knowledge, on his part, that if he is silent, or, still more, if he is critical, he will be regarded at best as a person upon whose loyalty no reliance can be placed. The United States has far too many trade unions whose real contact with Washington or the state capital is through a lobbyist; far too many unions, too, the minds of which speak not after their members have actively debated a question, but after some predominating figure in the union has decided what to say on their behalf; the assumption being that their main duty is to join in the chorus of applause following his solo performance. I should be the last to deny that Mr. John L. Lewis has brought great improvements in the working conditions of miners, as Mr. Petrillo has greatly increased the financial remuneration of the members of the American Federation of Musicians. But, speaking here with frankness, I am not able to believe that the benevolent despot in trade unionism has any creative validity which puts him in a higher category than the benevolent despot elsewhere. He feeds his sheep; there are obvious examples in which he feeds his sheep in rich pastures. The fact nevertheless remains that the sheep look to him to search for the pastures on their behalf. And when people tell me of the deep hold the benevolent despot in trade unionism has on the hearts of his men, proved, it appears, by the large salary, the immense car, or the palatial offices they vote him in appreciative gratitude, I cannot but think the process far too reminiscent of some "sawdust Caesar" in politics or industry.

In my view, therefore, it follows that trade unionism does not stop at the boundaries of the craft or industry within which it operates. That is why, to mention only the dead, the two American leaders whose careers have most impressed me are William H. Sylvis and Sidney Hillman. Sylvis was not only a great labor organizer and an ardent advocate of important social reforms: he saw these could be obtained only by the workers' direct participation in political life. His correspondence with leaders of the First International makes evident his anxiety to use the power of the workers for great ends which no easy revolutionism could hope to realize; and his eager efforts to set up trade-union reading rooms and lyceums are proof of his knowledge that the worker with the trained mind, who has learned how to look beyond the boundaries of his craft, is far more valuable to the community than the leader who makes his union his community, or the workman whose whole personality is absorbed in the most remunerative performance of his allotted task as ironmolder. I am glad to note that there are some signs that the achievement of Sylvis is winning from the historian a fuller recognition than was the case twenty, or even ten, years ago. It was his many-sidedness that made him a great man as well as a successful trade-union leader. It is the test of a trade unionist that, outside the special circle of his organization, he should have the power to win, if not agreement, at least respect, by integrating his professional life with other purposes in the fulfillment of which the stature of the whole community is raised. By that test it would be difficult to deny to Sylvis a success far more significant than that of many other trade-union leaders whose authority was wider than his and whose period of work lasted longer than the whole of Sylvis' brief life.

What Sidney Hillman did for his trade union others are far more competent to describe than I am. But I would like to note that, in doing it, he never failed to lay emphasis on three things. The union must know the technique of its industry at least as well as the employers it confronts; he put economic and technological research in the labor movement of America on a level which enabled the Amalgamated Clothing Workers to speak to management on something more than equal terms. He saw vividly the importance of providing its members with educational opportunities which did not leave them satisfied that the good life was fulfilled when there were higher wages and better conditions in the needle trades. The remarkable part he played in mobilizing the forces of labor to make sure of progressive victories in the elections of Franklin Roosevelt won for him a place in the confidence of the President which few other people attained; "he saw the whole range of our economic problems as perhaps only four or five other men in the United States," Mr. Roosevelt once wrote to me. In the American war effort he had that resolution and imaginative energy which enabled him to make a contribution of outstanding importance to our common victory over nazism. He was one of the major architects of that necessary World Federation of Trade Unions which we shall have to rebuild at the first moment after East and West have realized that great purposes cannot, on either side, be confined to the service of principles which become rigid dogmas when they are devoted to the aims of perverse propaganda. All this is achievement on the grand scale. But I want to add to it one touch of personal reminiscence. I well remember, during the course of an ugly blitz over London, talking to Mr. Hillman about the men whose friendship we had enjoyed in common ever since I was a youthful lecturer at Harvard University over a generation ago. He spoke with great warmth of President Roosevelt, of Mr. Justice Frankfurter, of that remarkable veteran in all great causes where it is urgent to protest against injustice, Mr. Charles C. Burlingham. Then he spoke for two or three minutes about Mr. Justice Brandeis, and he spoke like a man inspired. I no longer heard the foreign accent, which normally an Englishman could not fail to notice. I no longer heard those rough-hewn and jagged sentences which, when he used them, were always so effective and always so unpolished. He spoke like a man who had seen even beyond the vision of a great prophet. To my astonishment, he told me that as a young immigrant to America, painfully learning to speak English in some class, he had seen what his relations with Brandeis had emphasized overwhelmingly, that the supreme unmorality was to sacrifice the individual citizen to the harsh demands of the universe—and it was just as the all clear sounded, like the trumpet of triumph that it always seemed to be, that he asked me if I knew those lines of Shelley, which, since his teacher of English had first read them out to the class of immigrants, had remained with him as an unending inspiration:

> To suffer woes which Hope thinks infinite;
> To forgive wrongs darker than death or night;
>   To defy Power, which seems omnipotent;
> To love, and bear; to hope, till Hope creates
> From its own wreck the thing it contemplates;
>   Neither to change, nor falter, nor repent;
> This . . . is to be
> Good, great and joyous, beautiful and free. . . .

Never have I so acutely realized that if most trade-union effort is the dull prose of daily life, there are moments when it touches the supreme heights in the dreams of great dreamers.

I will add here only one other word, not in phrases of my own but in those of him who seems to me the man who saw most deeply into the hope we may look to from a trade unionism that is bold and experimental and thinks beyond the limits of job-control. In William Morris's words: "Take courage and believe that we of this age, in spite of all its torment and disorder, have been born to a wonderful heritage, fashioned of the work of those who have gone before us; and that the day of the organization of man is dawning. It is not we who can build up the new social order; the past ages have done most of that work for us; but we can clear our eyes to the signs of the times, and we shall then see that the attainment of a good condition of life is being made possible for us, and that it is our business to stretch out our hands to take it." [6] With the will and the imagination, that "good condition of life" is for trade unionism to make palpable and living. Our one enemy is the fear of seeking audacity as our ally.

[6] William Morris, *Signs of Change* (London, 1915), Collected Works, Vol. XXIII, p. 24.

II. TRADE UNIONS AND THE PUBLIC

1

IN THIS complex postwar world there is no industrial community at the heart of which the relation between trade unions and the public is not of pivotal importance. The smooth running of social life depends upon matters like transport, mining, agriculture, sanitation, the provision of a meat supply. If there is a breakdown in any of these industries—I have, of course, taken some obvious examples only— the threat it represents to the successful maintenance of urban life, especially in a great metropolis like London or Paris or New York, is literally overwhelming. That is why all industry that is directly clothed with a public purpose cannot involve itself in a major dispute without bringing the certainty, at some stage, most usually an early stage, of government intervention. It is not only true to say that the government will claim to intervene on behalf of the community; it is also true to say that there is a general expectation, where there is such a breakdown, that the government will intervene and that it is its duty to do so. Indeed, I think it is worth noting that the main criticism directed against the British government at the time of the general strike of 1926 was that it failed to take the appropriate measures to prevent the strike from occurring at all.

Certain historical changes that have occurred in this area of action are worth noting. The first is that only just over

fifty years ago the status of trade unionism was not sufficient
to make government intervention inevitable, nor did articulate opinion, at any rate, suggest that the government should
treat employers and trade unions on equal terms. When the
railroad managers persuaded Mr. Olney to act in the Pullman strike, it never occurred to him, still less to President
Cleveland, that the prelude to action should, in justice, have
been consultation also with Mr. Debs and the American
Railway Union. At almost the same time, to be precise, in
1899, the Postmaster-General of Great Britain consented, for
the first time, to receive written representations from a trade
union in the postal service, though it was not until 1906 that
he extended the right of recognition to such bodies. During
his first term as president, Theodore Roosevelt did not venture to fight the "coal barons" for the recognition of the
miners' unions in his effort to settle the dispute; indeed, the
President had to smuggle a labor representative into membership on his committee of inquiry, in the guise of a sociol-
ogist. Neither in the famous Ludlow strike of 1915 nor in the
steel strike of 1919 was there anything that can be called a
serious attempt by the federal government at Washington to
utilize its authority either to end the conflict or to secure the
kind of discussion out of which a settlement was likely to
emerge. In the Ludlow strike, it is not excessive to say that
the Rockefeller interests treated the President during most
of the time the strike lasted as an irrelevant, if important
outsider, not to be taken at his own valuation. It was only
after the revelation of the brutalities jointly sponsored by
the state militia and the Colorado Iron and Fuel Company
that the president of the latter was warned by Mr. Rockefeller's agent to treat the President with respect. In the steel
strike of 1919 Mr. Gompers appealed to President Wilson to
intervene; yet, anyone who scrutinizes with care the Presi-

dent's response can hardly avoid the conviction that it did far more to assist the United States Steel Corporation to win the strike than it did to create the atmosphere of settlement by discussion. To this it is fair to add that the state authorities, during the course of the strike, mainly acted as though they were the agents of the employers, and that, even after the grim revelations of conditions in the steel mills made in the now classic report of the Interchurch World Movement's Committee of Inquiry, some of the most influential newspapers in the United States opposed its recommendations—which are the commonplaces of industrial relations today—on the ground that the report "warped the facts in the interest of radical propaganda." [1]

What it is important to remember, as one analyzes the relations involved in all serious conflict between capital and labor, is that, save in the most exceptional circumstances, the trade unions, both in the objects at which they aim and the methods that if they are to avoid defeat they are bound to employ, compel action by the government at some level, and that this action will be overwhelmingly against any effort at change. For in a predominantly capitalist society the government is concerned with four things. It is concerned with the defense of law and order; foreign attack apart, this is the main ground upon which it claims to exercise the sovereign power of the state. It is concerned with securing to the community the continuous operation of vital services. Because it functions in a capitalist environment, it is concerned to protect the conception of freedom of contract which safeguards the worker's right, as an industrial member of the community, to work under the conditions

---

[1] By far the best account of the Ludlow and steel strikes will be found in the invaluable history by Professor Samuel Yellen, *American Labor Struggles* (New York: Harcourt, Brace, 1936), Chapters vii and viii. The quotation I have cited is given by Professor Yellen at page 290.

permitted by legislation. It is concerned, finally, to protect
the right of private owners of property to maintain the legal
relations inherent in the conception of private ownership,
save as these have been limited in any special direction by
the law. It follows, therefore, that where the trade unions
challenge any of these four conceptions, they are, in fact,
challenging the foundations of the state power; and the
unions are inevitably driven to this challenge immediately
they seek for objectives upon which there is not easy and
rapid agreement between themselves and their employers.

This is demonstrated clearly by the methods the trade
unions are bound to use in any major dispute. Apart from
appeals to the public, a trade union is bound to safeguard
itself against the scab by picketing; though the law permits
what it calls "peaceful" picketing, judicial records make it
obvious that the courts are not zealous about finding the
"peaceful" element in the picketing characteristic of a major
dispute. It is bound, also, to use the blacklist, the boycott,
both primary and secondary, and to seek the aid of other
unions relevant to a particular dispute by asking them to
strike in proof of sympathy and solidarity. The employer, on
his side, will, first of all, play for time in the sure knowledge
that this is the strongest weapon at his disposal. He will
seek the protection of his physical property and, where he
deems this urgent, he will ask that the police, or the militia,
or the army, be used for this purpose. He may decide to use
scab labor, in which case he will need to safeguard those
who accept such employment against the danger of violence
at the hands of those with whom his dispute has arisen.
There is need to take precaution against the risk of sabotage;
with the best goodwill in the world, the parties to any dispute cannot afford to overlook what angry men who feel
themselves wronged may attempt in the violence of their

indignation. The employer, too, must seek by propaganda to prove to the public that right is on his side; and he must not overlook the need for the support of his fellow employers, a support which may range from the passage of a resolution in a body like a Chamber of Commerce, through the attempt to bring organized pressure to bear upon any relevant level of government to use its public powers against the trade union and its supporters, to the creation, in their various forms, of vigilante committees to break the union by what is only too often the brutal use of illegal physical force. Additional complications arise when, as in the textile strike at Lawrence, Massachusetts, in 1912, there are competing unions in the industry one of which advises its members to take no part in the dispute which has arisen, or where some union which represents one craft in the industry is prepared, as in the American railroad strikes of 1877, to continue working while the other unions are on strike. Nor must one overlook the temptation, almost endemic in American industry, to create racial hostility, which is normally the immediate parent of violence, by using Negro labor to maintain production. That hostility is likely to be the more bitter since it has been the evil habit of far too many American trade unions to exclude the Negro from membership and thus to make of him a rival to be used as a weapon against them in any period of industrial difficulty. The trade union which discriminates between workers on the ground of color is bound, sooner or later, to fight the employer with weapons it has blunted through its own clumsiness.

For anyone with an elementary acquaintance with modern industrial history this too brief summary hardly needs serious documentary proof. Against some of the harsher results precautions have been taken both by legislation and by agreements between the trade unions and the employers.

Wages and hours of labor, for example, are now, in most areas of critical social importance, the subjects of statutory or voluntary agreements which establish minima and maxima respectively. In Great Britain the refusal to "recognize" a union for the purpose of collective bargaining is now the exception and not the rule in most important industries while in the United States the provisions of the Wagner Act have for close on fifteen years made impossible the kind of situation which President Theodore Roosevelt faced in the anthracite coal strike of 1902, or which the Ford Motor Company sought to preserve right down to the Second World War; the workers, that is to say, may compel their employer to recognize a trade union in which, by a free vote conducted under the auspices of the National Labor Relations Board, they express their desire to be organized; and the employer cannot, under the guise of propaganda, use the special authority inherent in his position to prevent the workers from joining that union if they so desire. Once the position of the trade union as the chosen agent for bargaining on behalf of the workers is established, the employer cannot refuse to deal with it in that capacity, though, of course, this does not mean that negotiations cannot break down. Since the passage of the Wagner Act in 1935, moreover, an employer cannot discriminate against any of his workmen by reason of his trade-union membership; one of the outstanding achievements, in short, of the National Labor Relations Board has been the outlawing of the notorious yellow-dog contract. No such elaborate machinery to protect the right of workers not only to have a trade union, but to have a union of their own choosing, exists in Great Britain or in any other representative democracy, at least to my knowledge; on the other hand, it is broadly true to say that union recognition and the collective bargaining which is its necessary corollary have been accepted in such communities as an essential element in industrial organization.

It would take me too far afield to describe, much less to discuss, the range of intervention in the realm of freedom of contract which is now a normal characteristic of government in a representative democracy. That range, of course, is nowhere the same, though it could be shown to be built around a central framework of purposes which become increasingly uniform in character. What I am concerned with is to inquire into two things. What is meant, in the first place, when a government makes its decisions "in the name of the community"? What is meant, in the second, when it is asserted that certain steps can, or cannot, be taken because of "public opinion"? From this second question, moreover, there arises a third: What exactly is this "public opinion" to which, where deemed necessary, the government, the employers, and the trade unions all alike appeal? We know, for example, that some of us would not be surprised if, during the course of an important industrial dispute, we saw a full-page advertisement in a newspaper in which the employers stated the case for the stand they were taking; we should leap up in amazement if, on the next day, we saw an answer to the employers' advertisement in the shape of a similar advertisement, in the same newspaper, arguing the case for the trade union. Most of us have been to public demonstrations, great and small, at which strikers, whether leaders or members of the rank and file, have put their case from the platform. Most of us, also, have seen a little file of men or women carrying notices informing us that a factory or a shop or a restaurant is guilty of unfair practices and, usually, asking us not to deal with it. Only recently I saw a long procession of the women who clean the offices in the great government buildings in Whitehall; they were marching, with a

kilted piper at their head, to protest against the refusal of Sir
Stafford Cripps, the Chancellor of the Exchequer, to agree to
their demand for an increase in their hourly wage rate. And
I have often stood in the central lobby of the House of Commons and watched not only members of trade unions on
strike, but also non-members in sympathy with them, inter-
view singly or in little groups members of Parliament whom
they hoped to influence in their favor. In most industrial
disputes in Great Britain, moreover, it is usual for both sides,
as well as members of the general public, to write to the
press for and against the disputants, or even in quest of
information.

The Government intervenes in industrial disputes on behalf of the "public." What is that "public" on whose behalf
it intervenes? In the larger number of its interventions in the
trade-union history of the United States the result of its
intervention has been the victory of the employers. Sometimes that has occurred through the use of the state militia
or of federal troops; sometimes it has been the outcome of
judicial decisions. And it is worth recalling that in all the
classic American strikes, from the disordered anger of the
railroad strikes of 1877 to the textile strikes in Gastonia in
1929 and that ugly Chicago strike of 1936 which the La Follette Committee on Civil Liberties investigated so carefully,
though strikers have been killed and jailed and fined, I think
I am right in saying that there is not a single case in which
an employer has had to answer to the law for the part he
and his major officials have played in what has often been
conduct no government should have tolerated for a moment.
Do not think that I am arguing, for one moment, that,
taking the record as a whole, the British government has
done better. No one who has looked at the Home Office
papers from the eighteen-thirties onward will have any illu-

sion about the issue. If Chicago has reason to be ashamed of the trial of the anarchists, the Whig government has deep stains, like the trial of the Tolpuddle Martyrs in 1831, on its escutcheon. There is not very much to be said for Mr. Asquith's use of the troops against the miners at Featherstonehaugh; and I do not suppose that Mr. Churchill's biographer will find the episode at Tonypandy one of the brighter spots in his long, and so often shining, career. Not since the savage anti-legislation against the working class from the time of Pitt to the time of Peterloo has a British government put on the statute book an Act of Parliament so deliberately vindictive as the Trade Union Law Amendment Act of 1927. It is notable, first, that when it was repealed in 1946 the House of Lords, though with ill grace, did not venture to delay the repeal. It is notable, second, that Mr. R. A. Butler, one of the most attractive and progressive of the Conservative leaders, has nevertheless pledged to the "public" the intention of his party, should it win the next general election, to re-enact those clauses which were thought so vindictive in 1927. With an irony that Mr. Butler is much too able to use unconsciously, he calls this re-enactment setting the trade unions free to perform their economic function.[2]

I agree at once that a long strike or lockout in any industry of major public significance causes at least inconvenience, often hardship and serious economic loss, to those who depend upon continuity of service in that industry, and that these dependents may well be, as in a great railway strike, for example, an important proportion of the whole community. I agree, further, that in a general way a government which is defending its people against external aggression, as in the War of 1939, is normally entitled to prohibit the stoppage of essential services. But I am bound

[2] Broadcast of Feb. 19, 1949, on behalf of the Conservative party.

to remark that the usual result of government intervention in a strike is to put the state power on the side of the employers, and thus to assure their victory. Take, for example, the Homestead strike. Both the state government and the federal government were well aware that the use of strike-breakers, even if all of these had been men of noble character, was bound to result in violence. No government could have been unaware that the use of armed guards, the swearing in of company employees as auxiliary police, the formation of vigilante committees, the wholesale organization of espionage by corporations against the trade unions, would lead to violence. They were employed because, once they led to violence, the intervention of the government against men on strike, and, as a rule, their defeat, was assured. No one can miss the plain significance of the way in which Governor Altgeld denied, in the Pullman strike of 1894, that the presence of federal troops was necessary. We never hear that a government forbids a company to buy tear gas or machine guns, or to use groups of armed thugs whose habits of mind and methods bear a grim resemblance to the Fascist bands of Mussolini and the stormtroopers of Hitler before either of them was able to seize power.

I freely admit that violence has often been used by the trade unions. The Sheffield outrages, the "Molly Maguires," the ruthless cruelty deliberately organized by union leaders against men who would not join their organization, the use of dynamite, as by the McNamara brothers in Los Angeles, these things, and many like them, make up a terrible tale. But I am bound to record my own view that most trade-union violence—jurisdictional disputes apart—has been due either to the denial of collective bargaining by the employers or to the fact that there is no level at which the power of government has not been used to protect employers' incitement to violence by men or acts organized for that purpose. In the textile strike at Lawrence, for example, it is very difficult not to conclude that the dynamite found in a tenement house in Oak Street, and elsewhere, was not deliberately put there either with the knowledge of the American Woolen Company or of the police; and it is startling to find that when the culprit, who was shown to be in close contact with the mill owners, was convicted for the act it was hoped would be attributed to the strikers, he was merely fined for the offense.[3] It is, quite honestly, pretty difficult to find, either in the United States or Great Britain, magistrates and judges on the one hand, or police on the other, who act with equal justice between employers and strikers.

There are occasions, moreover, when there is no strike and employers take industrial decisions which affect profoundly the lives of the workers without the government even attempting to compel the employers to show some sense of public responsibility. When Mr. Ford, faced with serious competition from General Motors and other corporations, decided that he must replace his famous model by a more modernized version, he turned thousands of his workers out of their jobs, to fend for themselves as best they could, without regard to what might happen to them. Anyone who knows the history of the "hiring halls" for longshoremen in American ports, and in British ports too until during the Second World War Mr. Ernest Bevin introduced the guaranteed week, cannot but be aware that they were nothing so much as breeding places of petty tyranny and corruption under the patronage of the employers. The unblushing autocracy of what are called "company towns" was well displayed in the New Deal era when Miss Frances Perkins, then Secretary of Labor in President Roosevelt's cabinet, found that

[3] Yellen, *op. cit.*, pp. 381-83.

the only place where she was permitted to speak was the steps of the Federal Post Office Building. Miss Perkins could return to Washington unhurt and without being arrested. But the experience of many trade-union officials who have been sent to try to introduce trade unionism into company towns, or into tragic areas such as those where the share-croppers of the South scrape up a miserable existence, is a record of death, of brutal injury, or of being run out of town or state under humiliating conditions which are far too often a deliberate violation of the American Constitution and for which there is no effective redress.

For all this, as I have said, we are given, mostly, two reasons. The first is that the government must protect the public, usually with the addition that it must safeguard law and order; and the second is, especially where no one industrial dispute is involved, that it must not invade the rights of property. Each part of the first reason deserves analysis. When it is said that the government must protect the public, what do the two words "protect" and "public" mean? By "protect" it cannot possibly be meant that the government of a modern community must prohibit any strike or lockout in a vital industry. For, first of all, there is no legal authority for saying that a strike called in contemplation, or furtherance, of a trade dispute is criminal, not even, I venture to add, if it is a general strike, like the British general strike of 1926. For when Viscount (then Sir John) Simon argued that a general strike like that of 1926 is "a strike against the general public to make the public, Parliament, and the government do something," [4] the central issue is not whether the public or Parliament or the government is involved, but whether it is a "simultaneous cessation of work on the part

[4] Sir John Simon, *Three Speeches on the General Strike* (London: Macmillan, 1926), p. 9.

of the workers" [5] who go on strike in furtherance of a trade dispute. Until the Trade Union Law Amendment Act of 1927, the fact that many of the strikers were not directly concerned with the dispute but came out in sympathy with the miners made no difference whatever to their legal right to strike; and the fact that they sought to put pressure on the public or Parliament or the government, on behalf of the miners, made no difference, legally, at all. In this context, the public, Parliament, and the government, are legally implicated only by the fact that the strike was in furtherance of a trade dispute. Once the question is put in that proper form in which Lord Simon, whether consciously or no, failed to put it, all the solemn edifice of his reasoning, influential as it was at the time, falls to the ground. The proper question is whether all or any of those who "simultaneously ceased" to work were guilty of treason or treason felony, of seditious conspiracy or seditious libel, or of criminal conspiracy at the time they struck, and granted the facts which surrounded the strike. The answer, quite obviously, is in the negative in all of these categories. It was only given the appearance, in each case, of being a crime by the use of words extended metaphorically to suggest that the strikers were deliberately engaged in harming the community by methods other than those of moral pressure. And this view is, I suggest, more than borne out by the second clause of the Emergency Powers Act of 1920. There it says specifically two things: first, that when a state of emergency exists—and this is defined as a proclamation by the government that the community or some substantial part of it is in danger of being deprived of the essentials of life—no regulations may be made authorizing any form of compulsory military service or industrial conscription; and, second, that no regulations under the Act

[5] *Farrer* v. *Close,* L.Q.B. 602, 612 (1869).

shall make it an offense for anyone to strike or peacefully to persuade other people to take part in a strike.

Except, therefore, where it is otherwise specifically provided for by statute, "protection of the community" by the government has no legal meaning and has never been given any legal meaning. Politically it is an expression of the view that every government must do the best it can for its citizens. No doubt the social philosopher can show grounds why this ought to be the case. That it is not the case over large areas of the world and has only exceptionally been the case in most ages I do not need to prove in detail. "Protect," in actual fact, has meant "protect within the permissible limits of the system approved by the ruling class," and the permissible limits only too often mean that there is no protection, or far too little of it. What does the Fourteenth Amendment to the American Constitution mean to an ordinary Negro worker in Georgia? What does freedom of assembly mean to the pecan nut-shellers in San Antonio, if the local police join hands with the local employers to prevent it? I do not forget that there is an important succession of recent cases in which the Supreme Court of the United States has by a majority thrown a wide arm of protection over the picketing process in industrial disputes and related it, in a deeply interesting way, to a right to freedom of speech which the Court will not permit a state legislature to invade, provided that what is said does not become "continuing representations unquestionably false." But I think it is important to bear in mind what Mr. Justice Jackson said in his dissent, concurred in by Chief Justice Stone and Mr. Justice Frankfurter, in *Hunt* v. *Crumboch* (see p. 17).

The American government, he argued in effect, since 1940, has used its duty to "protect the public" to mean that the majority of the Supreme Court protects trade unions against statutes by which states like Alabama and Illinois have sought to restrict trade-union activity. But it must be remembered that for many years before 1940 the Supreme Court "protected the public" by using the "due process" clause to make the employers its beneficiaries; and that in 1946 the Taft-Hartley Act sought by congressional legislation to put large restrictions on the gains of which Mr. Justice Jackson spoke in his dissent, written in 1945. Since President Truman's remarkable victory in 1948, won, in part at least, on the pledge that the Taft-Hartley Act would be repealed, there has emerged the prospect of a vivid discussion of just what in the Act should be repealed, and, even more, supposing it to be repealed, just what powers the President will assume, subject to what the Supreme Court may say in a particular case, to be inherent in his presidential authority. It is not, therefore, evasive to say that no one can really predict where the boundaries of the duty to "protect the public" will be in the future. It will partly depend on the outlook of the President. It will partly depend upon whether he can carry Congress with him. It will partly depend, also, upon the composition of the Supreme Court—and it is by no means certain, as some notable examples in our time have shown, that the members of the Court will remain consistent in their convictions throughout their period of service. In the generation since Woodrow Wilson became President for the first time, I am tempted to argue that Mr. Justice McReynolds and Mr. Justice Butler were the only two members of the Court about whose views one could make a prediction with some assurance before the hearing of the case began.

I think, therefore, that meaning is given to the phrase "protection of the public" by the balance of power in that conflict of economic forces which has haunted the American scene in different forms since 1789. Sometimes it has found its substance principally in the struggle between the trade unions and the employers; sometimes it has been shaped by the fight between the farmers and the railroads, or by that Populist movement in which the farmers have always been an essential element; sometimes it has been defined by the widespread fear of those great corporations, which, in Elihu Root's famous phrase, are the "invisible government" of the United States, even though they may use men like Senator Platt of New York, or Senator Quay of Pennsylvania, as their instruments. The battle may shift now a little one way, and now a little another. The important thing, over the whole campaign, is that until the great depression "protection of the public," despite the Interstate Commerce Act, the Sherman Act, the Federal Trade Commission, the Federal Reserve Board, and the Clayton Act, meant the victory of the employer over the trade union, the victory of the industrialist and the railroad over the farmer, the victory of the big corporation over the small business firm, the centralization of American economic power in comparatively few giant financial corporations. Since the great depression, the New Deal, aided by an angry and dismayed people, put a number of important curbs, like the Securities and Exchange Act, the Public Utility Holding Company Act, the National Labor Relations Act, and the Fair Labor Standards Act of 1938, upon the amazing power of finance capital to use "protection of the public," the formalities of the Constitution apart, as, quite simply, the protection of finance capital from invasion; and to these curbs, even before the election of Franklin Roosevelt, must be added the important victory won over the use of the injunction by the passage of the Norris-La Guardia Act. Taken together, all these, representing an invasion of the sovereignty of finance capitalism in the United

States, have given the trade unions a new significance in its economic life. But it is of immense importance not to exaggerate the degree to which this new significance has been permanently consolidated as a gain. We must wait to see if in the next years the principle of full employment can be maintained not merely without war, but without those fantastic armaments the cost of which is one of the major obstacles to the development even of the implications of the social service state. It has yet to be shown that what Thorstein Veblen called "trading on the national integrity . . . quite legally and morally under democratic forms" [6] may not be resumed under the shadow of external danger, and that its result may not be, to use another phrase of Veblen's, "a penalized subservience of its underlying population at home." Most of the effective agents of propaganda, the cinema, the radio, the press, and the pulpit, are ready enough to assist those vested interests the power of which has been temporarily arrested by a new dynamic in the trade unions for which Franklin Roosevelt did so much to find an adequate institutional expression. But it will require a good deal more thinking on the part of the workers before it can be said with assurance that the dynamic will be sustained.

The second cause to which I drew your attention is the need to protect that almost mystical conception which we call law and order, without the security of which, as Adam Smith said, the owners of property could not sleep soundly in their beds. It is obvious enough that once we penetrate beyond the superficial appearances of our society, its basic character is set by its productive relations, and that these are the outcome of the fact that the ownership of property is overwhelmingly in private hands. The result of this is, of

[6] Thorstein Veblen, *Absentee Ownership and Business Enterprise in Recent Times* (New York: B. W. Huebsch, 1923), pp. 422-23.

course, that disputes between employers and trade unions are, so to say, a disease of industry, and that the character of industry is given by the nature of ownership. But the nature of ownership does not include the right to work, still less the right to be safeguarded against the loss of work. Both of these are what the eminent legal philosopher, Hans Kelsen, has called "metajuridical conceptions," which become, or do not become, law in the degree that those who claim them have organized sufficient power behind their claims to get the recognition for them of statutory enactment or judicial decision. But it is always held that they threaten law and order if they seek to get them by force. Nearly every government that has not created an overwhelmingly socialist society assumes that force is, by nature, the use of police, or the militia, or the army, to safeguard physical ownership, of a factory, for example, from attack in an industrial dispute. It is significant that few American corporations are denied a license to purchase arms for the defense of their property, and that almost all the detective agencies which supply guards to the corporations are able, also, to obtain them. It is notable, too, that the right to call on the service of the armed forces at the disposal of government, at its different levels, is normally and naturally regarded as a proper prerogative of the ownership of some physical property that is held to be in danger.

We should not forget the occasional exception. Governor Altgeld tried to limit this prerogative of ownership in the Pullman strike. Governor Olson, in the teamsters' strike in Minneapolis, and Governor Murphy, in the automobile strike in Michigan, fought with remarkable courage against attempts to drive them into giving to ownership its prerogatival claim to the power to call for force to break up the opposition to its right to do what it willed with its own.

In the widespread sit-down strikes of 1936 President Roosevelt met with what he called "the old cry of the Tories: 'Something drastic must be done to curb labor; it is getting too powerful.'" His own comment is of deep interest. "I consider," he wrote, "the calling out of troops during a strike, except in a national emergency, one of the most dangerous things that can happen in a democracy. . . . I have always felt proud and gratified that during my service as Governor of New York, and as President of the United States, up to June 1941, after the full, unlimited national emergency had come, I have not once called out the militia or the troops in a labor dispute." [7] This outlook cost Altgeld his career. Olson died too soon for us to know how it would have affected his destiny; Mr. Murphy lost the governorship of Michigan, and owed his appointments both as Attorney-General of the United States and as Justice of the Supreme Court to the support of Franklin Roosevelt. Mr. Roosevelt, by reason of American entrance into the Second World War, was able to maintain his position unchallenged.

I think most people would be surprised if the trade unions sought to purchase modern weapons for self-defense on the scale we know that it is customary for the great corporations to do. We should be overwhelmed if a great trade union, in an industrial dispute, asked for, much less received, the aid of the police or the militia or of the federal troops to safeguard it in a claim to the right to work which it argued was as real as the physical right to visible and corporeal property, like a factory; and, if the right were to be recognized, I suspect that the courts would be ready to find that it was unconstitutional. The right to work is not formalized into a negotiable instrument which a judge will uphold

[7] *The Public Papers and Addresses of Franklin D. Roosevelt* (New York: Random House, 1938), Vol. III (1937), pp. 273-74.

as a prerogative of ownership no more to be invaded than the factory, the machines, and the materials of production, which can be seen and touched and felt. Once a job has been given, it may have, under law, to be paid for at a minimum price; but, once again, the right to maintain this as durable property, with special prerogatives of its own, is, as yet, very far from the status which ownership in the physical sense has won without any serious difficulty. The trade unions have to think of governmental policy, at least in a normal way, in very different terms.

2

The second reason we are given for the government's decision, in an industrial dispute, to intervene as it has been accustomed to do, is that it must not invade "the rights of property." You will observe these are spoken of as though they were some fixed and unchangeable substance an alteration in which would be shattering to the safety of the community. This is pure mythology which has not even the support of a pedigree sanctified by long tradition. The rights of property are always changing. They alter with place as they alter with time. I do not need to remind you that, since 1933, the American attitude to the rights of property has changed enormously. I agree, of course, that the idea that the protection of property from invasion by the power of numbers persists in the minds of most, at least, of those who make the fundamental decisions of our society. But the area over which that protection is extended has changed a great deal in the years between 1918 and 1945. Partly that is the outcome of revolution following war, partly it is the result of the effort to discover ways and means of avoiding revolution. Yet, even when full account is taken of what surrenders the rights of property have undergone, it still remains the fact that there is a very large area of action in which what the trade unionist may hope for is determined by the expectations of the owner of property which a government is prepared to satisfy.

What it is important to realize is that, almost as long as the memory of man, there has been an antithesis between the rights of property, which, in themselves, are merely the outcome of bare ownership unaccompanied by effort, and the rights of labor, which are based upon an effort personally made. In nothing so much is this visible as in the denial by the law of most states that property can be taken by the government, in the highest interests of the community, without the payment of compensation; where, on the other hand, it is rare to admit that a worker who may have invested the industrial skill of a lifetime in some particular enterprise has any title to compensation if the owner of the enterprise decides to dispense with his services. No doubt special exceptions exist, as in the case of war. But it is illuminating to note the attitude both of legislatures and of courts to the rights of property when land is taken for a public purpose, or when an industry is nationalized, or when the rate of some utility like a telephone company is lowered by the appropriate authority to a point below what Mr. Justice Brandeis has taught us to believe a conceptual "prudent investor" might legitimately have expected to receive. We even extend the rights of property to include the notion that the director of a corporation which is merged with another corporation is usually regarded as entitled to compensation for loss of office if the merger results in his exclusion from the new directorate that is established. We agree that a corporation's goodwill is also an asset for which compensation must be paid. We do not doubt that the owner of land under which are discovered mineral resources, of the existence of which he was unaware and for the development of which he has no means, has, nevertheless, the right to the protection of the state power. Nor do I need to remind you of the vast protection given to the owners of property under the Fifth and Fourteenth Amendments to the American Constitution; and of the immense addition to the wealth of those who live by functionless ownership whenever, in the monetary field, the government of some community decides, like Mr. Churchill when he was Chancellor of the Exchequer, upon a policy of deflation. To this it is important to add the protection afforded to the owner of property—apart from the creation of a nuisance—who either wholly or in part refuses to put it to productive use unless he is satisfied with the return he will secure from such use. He has the right to keep his land, or his factory, or his savings, all at his own discretion, even if this may mean unemployment or scarcity in the market. We are told that these rights of property must be protected because, if they are attacked, confidence in the community's secure future will break down, and that this will lead to economic and social disease. The protection of the state power afforded to the owner of property as a right he legitimately enjoys thus becomes a power in him, and others in a similar position, to hold the community to ransom. The right to property, even with the limitations imposed upon it by the condition of our times, thus becomes the right to determine how and when both the natural resources and the current technological knowledge of our time shall be employed. There is a limit set to our power to employ these to their full possibility by the right recognized in the owners by the state power to determine where the boundaries of their use shall be set.

Once the rights of property are protected in this way by

the state power in any community, the character of the protection afforded is bound to have a profound effect upon the possible achievements of the trade unions in that community. I do not need to insist that it was the power of property to organize society, to limit the satisfaction it was prepared to afford only to the effective demands that it encountered, that made the economy of the market, with its impersonal mechanism of price, so transcendent a factor in our lives. It is not less obvious that, once the right of property to enlarge or to diminish the risks it was prepared to make was admitted, it was quite natural for the courts to hold, as in the famous Mogul case [8] in England, that owners could do with impunity what it would have been regarded as conspiracy for workers to attempt. It is fascinating to note the amazement with which legal opinion received the famous dissent of Mr. Justice Holmes, then on the Supreme Court of Massachusetts, in *Vegelahn* v. *Guntner* in 1896,[9] when he argued to the majority of his brethren that peaceful picketing was lawful and told them that since "competition on the one side is patent and powerful, combination on the other side is the necessary and desirable counterpart if the battle is to be carried on in a fair and equal way." Not less striking was his view that it was "lawful for a body of workmen to try by combination to get more than they are now getting . . . and to that end to strengthen their union by the boycott and the strike." [10] These dissents are the more striking because Holmes was a conservative in matters of economic philosophy and thoroughly accepted, I suspect, the doctrine of the wages fund, even then a pretty obsolete doctrine among serious economists. His effort to insist that if

[8] L.Q.B. 1 (1894).
[9] 167 Mass. 92 (1896).
[10] *Plank* v. *Woods*, 176 Mass. 492 (1900).

competition is to be free it must be waged on equal terms
between employers and trade unions stands in striking contrast to the almost contemporary Taff Vale Railway case in
England, in which Mr. Justice Farwell, subsequently upheld
by the House of Lords, had no difficulty in finding that when
Parliament said that a trade union shall not be responsible
for the tortious acts of its agents, it really meant that a trade
union shall be responsible since there was no clear evidence
that Parliament consciously intended to repeal that famous
maxim of the Common Law that the principal is responsible
for the tortious acts of his admitted agent.[11] That case is not
really less remarkable than the decision of the House of
Lords in the famous Osborne case, in 1911, when the House
of Lords upheld Mr. Osborne's contention that it was no
part of the function of the trade unions to pay men to represent them in the House of Commons on the ground that
this financial connection was clearly contrary to public policy; at a generation's distance, the opinion of Lord Shaw of
Dunfermline has really to be read to be believed. It must be
remembered that this came from the court which had accepted the view that trade competition carries its own justification so long as it seeks self-interest and profit. But since
trade competition does not legally include the competition
between capital and labor, as a result, labor is responsible
for any damage it may do to others by seeking self-interest
and profit through the application of economic pressure. It
is obvious that the House of Lords did not differ from most
American courts—with notable exceptions like that of the
Supreme Court of Massachusetts in the Holmes period and
the Court of Appeals in New York in that brief but remarkable period when Judge Parker was its main figure—in its

[11] See W. M. Geldart, *The Present Law of Trade Disputes and Trade
Unions* (London: Milford, 1914).

anxiety to put the rights of property far ahead of the rights of trade unions.

It is interesting to note that in 1921, when the Lloyd George government organized British railways into four great systems, it was laid down that any further amalgamation should be followed, under specified conditions, by compensation to men whose skill was rendered unnecessary by that action; but it is not less interesting that, a few years later, when the four systems set out to make large-scale pooling arrangements, through the operation of which they were able to save a considerable amount of skilled manpower, they dismissed men long in their employ. They were allowed to insist that this was a mere "pooling arrangement" and not an amalgamation, and that therefore they were in no wise bound to pay any compensation to the men whom they laid off. It is even more significant that in most countries, in Professor Louis Hacker's phrase, the small and tenant farmer is doomed. He is mostly held within the vise of a complex framework of credit, salesmanship, or markets to which he is never certain of direct access. He must provide the necessary return on the capital of those to whom he owes for the equipment he must buy, even for things like the chemicals he increasingly requires, so that his rights become every year more certainly the result of what is left when their rights have been satisfied. And if he is not running a family farm, but is dependent on hired workers to run it, the hired workers are, in their turn, the residuary legatees of what he can manage to save from a system in which he is increasingly being pushed to the wall. The pathetic result is written grimly in the history of farm mortgages, the decline of tenant farming, and the unmistakable fact that measures for his relief, like the Triple A Act, do far more to help the big man than they do the small. The only sense in which the agricultural market belongs to the small farmer is that he cannot really escape from the prices forced upon him by immense business interests it is quite beyond his power to control.

It is an inevitable outcome of the place given to the rights of property by the state power that the trade union is, in all but the most abnormal conditions, put into a secondary place. For it is those who manage a business who initiate responsible action, make decisions about sales and advertising, and determine, within the limits given to them by the market within which they operate, not only what they shall charge for the commodities they sell, but also, in the situation they confront, whether combination or competition will suit them better. For it is always important to remember that the price system which the market involves is not an effort to manufacture more commodities but an effort to make more money. In the market economy of the modern capitalist community all the rights of property cohere about this effort as its central principle, to the point where it has become almost a routine element in business enterprise. The major mechanisms, indeed, of finance capitalism are all directed to dragging more deeply behind the protective armament of the state power such devices as the holding company, the interlocking directorate, and the type of reorganization in which the late J. P. Morgan was so remarkable a performer—a grouping of previously competing enterprises into a new and unified combination with a capital at once beyond their total market value and far greater than the sum of the value of the total physical assets they possessed. These, therefore, almost invariably overcapitalized, were usually weighted down with a burden of overhead charges their annual earnings could hardly hope to meet; with the result that, at least until the controlling legislation of the New Deal period, once reorganization was complete, they had rarely any choice, not least in key industries like railroads, coal, and steel, between seeking an increase in price of the commodity or service they produced, or an attack upon wages and other labor conditions. It was thus natural enough for them to be anxious to avoid the recognition of trade unions lest the massed force of the workers should make the second choice impossible.

For what all this has worked out to since the twentieth century began is that the sense of confidence upon which the successful conduct of business depends, the ability, therefore, of any corporation which is of importance to avoid bankruptcy and to secure the credit which enables it to keep up with swiftly changing technological conditions—it being understood that, normally, serious technical obsolescence means industrial death—depend upon the goodwill of the bankers. They operate, no doubt, within boundaries approved by the Federal Reserve Board and the Securities and Exchange Commission; but the degree to which their common objective is to preserve confidence by maintaining stability in the realm of finance means that power is ever more centralized in these groups, and that the swifter the pace of technological improvement, the greater will be the degree of centralization. Save in very exceptional cases, the more complete will thus be the dependence of the manufacturing corporation or the farmer upon the credits obtainable from the banking community in order to obtain the credits which enable the units of industry and farming not merely to improve, but even to maintain, their position in the markets they are compelled to act in as relevant to their operations. When, therefore, we say that the initiative in industrial or agricultural strategy lies with management in industry, we mean, in fact, that this initiative can be exercised by those who control the vital credit mechanism of the community. This is the point brought out so clearly in classic documents like the Report of the Pujo Committee and by the remarkable investigation of Wall Street in 1933–34 conducted by the Senate Committee on Banking and Currency with the powerful counsel of Judge Ferdinand Pecora. It is where this ultimate initiative is centralized that the rights of property are effectively determined.

In my view, the character of this initiative is primary, and that of the trade unions secondary, in importance. The trade unions, in so far as they make job-control their major concern, must rely upon a rhythm of conduct which is not effectively independent, but, in the main, adapted to that of the interests with a private initiative. Beneath all the rhetoric of the labor movement lies the urgent fact that trade-union demands are an effort to secure better conditions, especially of wages, from corporations whose habits are set by their domination by the men who operate the mechanism of credit. In the market economy the trade union functions on the model of the business corporation. It tries by a body of well-known rules—from the closed shop, through the limitation of output, to the control of the number of apprentices permitted to the skilled craftsman—to make the commodity, labor power, it has to sell as scarce as possible. If it is so strategically placed that it can secure an increase of wages for its members, that increase is expressed in terms of price. But the price of any given worker's increase in wages is necessarily reflected in the general level of prices; and if an increase in wages for a large enough group of workers affects that price level, it means that consumers' goods cost more. Since this, of course, diminishes the reality of the increase the workers concerned have received, the trade unions fol-

low, and do not determine, the initiative and the authority
inherent in the rights of property. The government of the
community will, no doubt, seek as best it can to prevent that
initiative and authority from being used so aggressively and
intolerably as to threaten the foundations of law and order.
But those foundations are best understood if they are
regarded as the conditions in which there is business confidence and the maintenance of continuity in market prop-
erties. Where these are absent, the economic life of the
community is threatened. The government then, either by
force or by persuasion, prevents that threat from reaching
the point of danger. To do so it must maintain the rights of
property, which rest ultimately, as I have sought to show, in
the hands of the small group of men who control the credit
mechanism of the society; and, to the extent of that maintenance, it is bound to be an instrument on the side of the
status quo. It is the knowledge that it is such an instrument
which, in the long run, transforms any trade union the offi-
cers of which are seriously concerned to improve their members' standard of life not merely into claimants, on ordinary
business principles, for a larger share of whatever stock of
welfare there is; it turns them, also, if they are honest, into
men ready to fight the employers for the larger share to
which they lay claim; and, in extreme issues, where, as in
the British general strike of 1926, a claim for better conditions becomes accepted as a demand, passionately felt, for
what is held to be social justice, into men ready to use all
the power they have against the government which, by protecting the rights of property, is bound to appear to them as
their enemy. The logic of the assumptions upon which the
private ownership in the means of production rests never
seems permanently natural or just to trade unionists who

understand that they are, in fact, even when at peace, involved in a relation to their employers which is properly described as merely the conduct of war by other means.

3

It is here, I think, that the vital question arises of the relation of the trade unions to politics in the modern state. More and more, it is bound to assume the shape of a decision between remaining, as in the United States, a pressure group, seeking to bring what influence they have to bear on political parties from which, as trade unions, they stand apart, or becoming, like the trade unions in Great Britain, the basis of a political party which, founded in 1899 in alliance with a number of socialist societies, became in 1945 the majority party in the House of Commons. Though the Labour party, as a minority, had been in office twice before, in 1924 and 1929, in 1945 its overwhelming victory (394 seats out of 640) enabled it to put forward the whole of its election program as the basis of its legislation. The Labour government has already nationalized the Bank of England, the coal mines, the electric power and gas industries, the railroads, and long-distance road transport. It has reorganized the medical profession and the private and local hospitals into an almost complete national health service, which includes the dental and optical aspects so gravely neglected until this measure. It has provided also the greatest scheme of social insurance, with immensely increased benefits, there is in the world today, including, in particular, children's allowances, maternity benefits, provision against unemployment, and security in old age. Its housing program has been both larger and more successful than any others; and its policy of rationing all commodities which are in short supply, while it has not prevented that regime of austerity which both the financial cost and the physical devastation of the war would in any case have made inevitable, has at least had the immense merit of preventing the main necessities of life from being distributed with gross unfairness between the wealthy and the poor. If the next general election takes place in 1950, the Labour government will also have completed the nationalization of the steel industry and reduced the power of the House of Lords to delay the passage of vital measures of social reform from two years to one. I shall not here discuss the international policy of the Labour government. But I think it is important to note that it has helped India, Pakistan, and Ceylon to achieve a self-government as free and as full as that of Canada, Australia, and New Zealand, and that it has acquiesced in the wish of Eire and Burma to be released from any relations with the British Commonwealth of Nations.

When the last criticism has been made, I think it is very difficult to deny that all this represents an outstanding achievement. For it has been accomplished by the government of a nation brought to the verge of disaster by six years of financial loss and physical devastation in the Second World War, the outbreak of which had afforded no real opportunity to recover from the heavy loss of the War of 1914. I know, of course, that much of its work, not least its complete repeal of the Trade Union Law Amendment Act of 1927—which roughly corresponds to the Taft-Hartley Act —has been angrily criticized by the Opposition, led by the great wartime leader of the British people, Mr. Winston Churchill, who, with the Conservative party he led, was so decisively defeated by the Labour party in 1945. I know also that the economic recovery of Great Britain and the prevention of what might have been a catastrophic fall in its standard of life have been dependent on the European Recovery Program, largely devised by Mr. Dean Acheson and sponsored by General Marshall when he was Secretary of State. But I think it is fair to offset that criterion by the high eulogies given to the effort of the British people, and its government, in testimony before congressional committees by Mr. Paul Hoffman, Mr. Averell Harriman, and Mr. Lewis Douglas, none of whom has ever shown any leaning to the Labour party or sympathy with its principles; and they are able, I think, to take a more detached view of its work than Mr. Churchill, who, after all, is anxious that its defeat at the next general election—an unlikely event, in my judgment— should result in his own return to Downing Street as Prime Minister.

I do not for one moment suggest that the example of the British Labour party is one that has universal validity; differences in national tradition and habits and circumstances obviously require methods of action suitable to those differences. But what I am anxious to maintain is the view that the acquisition of influence in politics by labor through its indirect action as a pressure group, whether on a narrow front as Mr. Gompers attempted, or on a front both broad and deep such as that attempted by the Political Action Committee of the CIO under Mr. Hillman's leadership, is unlikely to help the trade unions on the scale now necessary, as the formation of a progressive political party, built on the support of the trade unions, would be capable of achieving. This attitude is not regarded with general favor in the United States; that is why I have spoken of the need for a "progressive" party rather than one which is democratically socialist in outlook, like the Labour party of Great Britain. I admit that leading trade unionists and scholars, who, like Professor Selig Perlman, have given almost a lifetime of devoted effort to the study of American trade unions in action, remain strongly opposed to my view; for trade unionists of otherwise diverging views can join with leading representatives of business in the United States in urging that all the economic problems Americans are likely to confront in the foreseeable future can be solved within the framework of a capitalist society. I should like to explain why, from the standpoint of the trade unions, the confidence of their leaders in the methods of the pressure group is wholly mistaken.

I begin by pointing out that all trade-union problems which are not capable of being resolved by the normal processes of collective bargaining have become problems the satisfactory determination of which depends upon the ability of the trade unions to influence the government in Washington not less promptly than it is influenced by the pressure groups of business. Where the problems are not directly of a trade-unionist character, but, nevertheless, bear directly upon the welfare of the workers, social matters like the adequate provision of housing, or of low-cost medical care, or of satisfactory educational standards in the schools, or of equal aid to persons of low income groups who find themselves caught in the costly grip of the courts, there I should have thought it still more clear that the pressure group is wholly inadequate as an influence compared to the authority with which an important progressive party could speak. When we move to the largest aspects of public policy, the making of peace and war, foreign policy, fiscal arrangements, to take examples only, I doubt greatly whether any pressure group, at least on the labor side, will be able to make any impact on the decisions of the government in any profound way. Most pressure groups, where they are successful, secure their results partly in proportion to the money they spend and partly by the promotion of a narrowly specific objective they make widely understood both by governments and by public opinion. But most of the objectives at which the trade unions are aiming today are pretty closely interwoven with the general pattern of policy to which a government devotes itself. That has been true, I think, in the United States at least from the close of the First World War, and still more true since the great depression secured the election of Franklin Roosevelt to the White House. It is not enough, in order to be an effective trade unionist, to see problems merely in terms of a craft or of a job. For each problem is set in a context that requires decision on a mass of other questions reaching far beyond the boundary of any one of them. One has only to think of two issues of special contemporary importance—those of communism and the implications of the European Recovery Program—to see that this is so. And I need only mention the fact that every trade unionist is, qua trade unionist, bound to be intimately affected by the prospects of peace and war, and the scale of armaments those prospects involve, to make it plain beyond dispute that any clear separation is impossible between unionism looking solely to job-control and unionism recognizing that, at each stage of its activity, it is bound to touch on a dozen important matters about which it must have a policy and around which it must mobilize all the influence it is in its power to secure.

If this be so, the notion that it can be done by the Gompers method or even by the more dynamic and insistent approach embodied in the PAC of the CIO seems to me to fall to the ground. It has failed to realize the changed relations between democracy and economic power. It has no adequate insight into the degree to which the modern corporation, especially in an era of increasing social interdependence, needs to have the state power on its side if it is to defend itself from precisely the kind of pressure group with which,

since the period of Gompers' ascendancy, labor has been
content. If I may say so, it has been pretty rare since 1900
in America for the leaders of the trade unions frankly to admit the immense volume of sheer coercion that is required
to keep industrial capitalism an effective and going concern.
Where this necessary volume of coercion is so far challenged
as to seem in jeopardy, business, which is itself a system of
power, requires the government as its partner in order that
it may use the state power which the government operates.
It may seek, of course, to obtain control over the government
by peaceful means; if it cannot do so, then the cases both of
Mussolini and Hitler are only the major instances of our time
in which business and the state power become almost inter-
changeable terms. It is not accident that each of them moved
directly to the destruction of free trade unions, nor that this
destruction was also one of the major characteristics of
Vichy France. Nor is it accident that, in the aftermath of a
war which has put the control of the trade unions into Communist hands, French businessmen look more and more to
General de Gaulle to relieve them from a trade-union challenge which threatens what they believe to be the minimum
volume of coercion necessary to maintain the discipline of
the workers. This enables political democracy in large part
to conceal the fact that, granted the private ownership of the
means of production, political democracy is not seldom a
façade behind which the great corporations prepare a social
order the character of which is not unlike that of the corporate state. It is, moreover, worth noting that in Great
Britain practically all the important wartime controls of
industry were in the hands of men drawn from the great
corporations that were outstanding in their particular spheres
of production. It does not seem to me fantastic to suggest
that if the general election of 1945 had been won by the

Conservative party its victory would have been followed by serious industrial disputes, as was the case after the election of 1918. In that event, a Conservative Prime Minister, fresh from the organization of a great democratic triumph, might easily have found himself driven to maintain industrial discipline by the use of instrumentalities whose partnership with Hitler had lain at the very roots of the war.

I confess to a deep sense of disturbance at the refusal of the American trade unions to follow through the implications of this relation of organized economic power to democracy on its political side. The philosophy of American capitalism is still so set in a tradition that regards the state power as neutral, individualism in business as normal, and monopoly as an occasional deviation from the norm; it is still so widely held that class warfare belongs to Europe and not to America, and, even in Europe, to fanatics who cling to a Marxian historical analysis which serious students have long regarded as obsolete; that, despite remarkable work which has made this easy optimism largely irrelevant to the facts, the overwhelming tendency among trade-union leaders is to accept the view, ever more emphasized by the historian and the economist, that the circumstances of the American past, and the "way of life" to which it has given birth, make it in the highest degree unlikely that the tendencies so markedly hostile to democracy in Europe can obtain an effective hold in the United States. I hope, indeed, that those who take this view may prove right. I remark only that were a major depression suddenly to strike the American economic system, the trade unions could not meet its challenge by suddenly improvising an insistence that the state power should be tilted toward the protection of the workers and the "little men," as it was tilted by Franklin Roosevelt generally, if with moments of inconstancy, until the terrible shadow of the Second World War made it necessary for him to discover a *modus vivendi* with the leaders of Big Business. I agree with Professor Brady [12] that in a great industrial crisis the loyalty of the vested interests is less likely to be an acceptance of adjustment to the needs of the common people than a claim to the exclusive possession of sovereignty on its own account, its argument being that only in this way can it overcome the crisis by restoring "confidence"—that is to say, its own confidence in itself—and re-creating the conditions in which production may be maximized and, therefore, the largest possible volume of employment assured. I do not think that, under circumstances like those the next great crisis in American economic life may reveal, the huge vested corporate interests of America will seek earnestly to preserve the state power as neutral between opposing tendencies; but that they will consciously demand that for which they have so long prepared—the subordination of the state power to their own service in order to impose on the trade unions that authoritarian discipline they sincerely believe to be ever more urgent. In that event, I am entirely unconvinced that the organization of the trade unions as no more than one, or two, or even three pressure groups will prove even remotely adequate to redress the balance of state power. I do not believe that in any large-scale economic crisis capitalist civilization possesses a formula of action deliberately conceived to adapt its policies to democratic institutions. I am more convinced than I have ever been that the character of economic development makes it imperative that the government, with its right to exercise the sovereign power, must be in the hands of those who are prepared, at almost any cost, to preserve the essentially democratic character of govern-

[12] Robert A. Brady, *Business as a System of Power* (New York: Columbia University Press, 1943).

ment. In America, this can be seen in the attitude of the "economic royalists" to the really moderate legislation of President Roosevelt's New Deal, and in the skill with which, to enable him to win the war, those who had become at least his opponents found themselves able to put themselves inside some of the most vital agencies of President Roosevelt's own government. We learn the vital lesson that, since the scale and number of these new agencies put them outside the area of rigorous control by the President or Congress, there comes a point where administration does in fact become government; and its ability to operate under the authority of statute or regulation gives the agency all the power, and the President all the responsibility. The habits enforced, the traditions embodied in policy, are, most of them, the habits and conditions rejected by the people at five separate elections since 1932. Certainly, as yet, the trade unions, with a technique long outmoded on all the vital levels, have found no way of neutralizing the skill of the vested corporate interests which it is essential for them to attain. American democracy, when its trade unions operate mainly on the Tuesday after the first Monday of November, reminds me of nothing so much as the famous description by Rousseau of representative government in Britain. "The British People," he wrote, "are mistaken. They think they are free. But they are free only at election time." So the American people, reasoning that the government and the vested interests are increasingly one, ought through their trade unions to make sure that the sovereignty of the government, as an instrument of public welfare, cannot be diminished, without the full knowledge of the trade unions, into the instrument of the great corporate interests. How is that to be achieved?

Before I answer this question I ought to deal with a preliminary objection. "You argue," it may be said, "that the government and the vested interests are increasingly one. But in the United States there has been since 1933 a government critical of the vested interests, which the latter have proved unable to overthrow; while in Great Britain and in Scandinavia, as well as in Australia and New Zealand, there are democratic socialist governments engaged in transforming the capitalist foundations of society despite the strong opposition of vested interests, which, short of the use of violence, do everything in their power to arrest the process of transformation. How, then, can you argue that there is unity between government and the vested interests?" Upon this comment there are two remarks to be made. The first is that in all communities in which a socialist government, operating democratically, is in power, the boundaries of the changes it makes, and the speed with which it is able to make them, are set by its need to carry with it an important degree of cooperation from the vested interests. If an industry is nationalized, satisfactory compensation must be paid to the displaced owners. While nationalization may bring better conditions to the workers in an industry taken over by the government, there has not yet been devised anything like a satisfactory technique for the effective enhancement of the workers' status; an overwhelming proportion of the posts which carry with them power and responsibility remain, if not in the same hands as before, at least in the hands of men of the same type as before. The democratic community, with a socialist government in power, has moved—I agree that it is an important move—from private capitalism to state capitalism and has embarked on social reforms on a far larger scale than would be attempted in, say, a Great Britain in which the Conservative party was in power, or in a New Zealand in which the courageous government over which Mr. Peter Fraser presides was replaced by its opponents. The machinery of finance, the Bank of England, for example, apart, all the industries which have become publicly owned in Great Britain, the coal mines, the railroads, electricity, wireless communication, gas, will need immense capital expenditure to get them into a condition of high efficiency. The need for that capital expenditure not only means a crushing weight of taxation upon the middle class; it means also that the pace of urgent social reforms is slowed down in vital areas like health, education, the opening of the roads to culture and dignified leisure to the vast majority of the people. So long as those social reforms are slowed down, the major officials in all nationalized industries will continue to be drawn from a pretty small group; and, even though the ultimate power of direction over these officials will lie in the hands of a socialist minister responsible, through the cabinet, to Parliament, it will be many years before we can approach the position where we can say that we have got somewhere near equality of opportunity.

After five years of a Labour government the private sector of industry in Great Britain will still represent eighty per cent of the economy. There the motive to production will remain profit-making; the method of production will be the market economy, and any government largely dependent upon export will have to be careful not to disturb the confidence of the vested interests in the private sector, even to confirm them in their confidence of a large number of guarantees which are, so to say, the provision of social services to anti-socialist concerns. The vested interests have a political strategy fairly comparable to the political strategy of government. The government, as an instrument of social development, only keeps the initiative in the campaign by just enough social reform to keep hope alive in the trade unions on the one hand, without going so far as to drive the vested interests into counterrevolutionary effort on the other. And in a democracy this means that every few years the electorate must be persuaded to renew the power of a socialist government, since the risks involved in its defeat may mean that the vested interests will, by their victory, be able to undo an important part in the effort to move to socialism. Nor must I fail to note that a socialist state in a predominantly capitalist world must aim at unity between capital and labor in the private sector in order to put behind its needs of influence and power in the field of international relations the dynamic of authority which is the outcome of a unified economic order in which there are industrial peace and labor efficiency. A long strike, for example, in the automobile industry in Great Britain might easily, by the disturbance of its balance of trade, be fatal to a socialist government by rendering it unable to import commodities urgently needed to satisfy the expectations of the ordinary voter. A socialist government has, therefore, especially in a period of full employment, to beg the unions not to press for excessive wage increases; it asks, so far as possible, for a standstill on the wages condition. No doubt it asks also that the corporations shall not increase their dividends to their shareholders. The latter's response, for which it will exact high praise, still leaves dividends of fifteen per cent a normal occurrence; and there will be exceptional cases where an agreement not to increase dividends still leaves the gratified shareholders with from thirty to sixty per cent on capital, with the simultaneous sense that they are obviously by their sacrifice patriotic citizens.

A democratic socialist government, in a word, is always walking upon a razor's edge. Formally, the coercive power of the state is in its hands; actually, it knows perfectly well that it must not use it in such a way as to outrage the vested interests. That leads me to my second remark. A democratic socialist government retains its power because, by putting the economic interests of the trade unions into organized action on the political plane, it creates, slowly and a little clumsily, the conditions in which it can hope to absorb some economic power which threatens it, and to set other economic power in a context where a good deal of its effort to make the government its agent can at least be neutralized. The community in which a democratic socialist government exercises the state power must do what no liberal government was able to do—overcome the profoundly coercive power of industrial capitalism, thus enabling it to impose its decisions upon a minority that, previously, was able, despite the forms of democracy, to impose control upon a majority. I see no way of doing this except by putting the trade unions directly into politics and persuading them to make their purposes wide enough to attract support from other progressive elements in the community. It has been easier for the corporate power of wealth, at once so intensely concentrated and so diversely organized, to control political parties which are concerned less with the translation of principles into action than with acting as brokers of ideas which will, as they hope, sweep them into victory and thus place the spoils of office at the disposal of their supporters. A political party which is uninhibited by the possession of a philosophy is bound, sooner or later, to fall into the control of the most powerful vested interests in the community; and it is obvious that, in a society where the instruments of production are privately owned, the most powerful vested interests are those of property. Political parties cannot escape from the need to have an economic basis which determines their direction. If they are tied too loosely to that economic basis,

in place of the politics of policy we get the politics of stratagem; and the character of the stratagem is never maintained
for long by numbers in an unequal society; it is determined
by the power which attends upon property. That was seen
with exceptional clarity by the men who made the Constitution of 1787; and it was driven home with magistral incisive-
ness by the authors of the *Federalist*, and especially by James
Madison in the remarkable tenth paper in that work.

Already, in the United States, the trade unions have tried
to invoke the aid of government for their protection on a
scale, especially since the New Deal, which has made the
different variations upon the theme Mr. Gompers adopted
completely irrelevant. The trade unions are now directly related not merely to the national, but also to the international,
aspects of American policy. And the very scale of the new and
vast governmental agencies which have grown up since Mr.
Roosevelt came to power means that the degree of their
operation will largely determine the volume of employment
in New Deal democracy. No trade unions can fail to see that
this directly involves them in politics to a degree far beyond
the simple theory of labor as one pressure group among
many others. Nor, I venture to think, is this likely to be less
apparent when American foreign policy involves the government not merely in institutions which seek for political
methods to secure collective security, but also in an immense
growth in the defense establishments, and, therefore, both in
their costs and their right to call for the use of manpower in
the service of defense, without which defense has little or
no meaning in the context of collective security. The growth
of the scale of government and the acceptance of the policy
of collective security both mean that economic interests have
to find their appropriate political institutions. If the trade
unions become more than only tangentially related to these,

it follows that they must seek directly to permeate them with their own outlook. That means more than the abandonment of a market mechanism supposedly working out the delicate equilibrium between production and effective demand. It calls for the recognition that "free enterprise" is nowadays a mythological concept no longer relevant to the issues before us. There is a world of difference between Adam Smith's "simple system of natural liberty" and the dynamic pattern of a new technology which has hardly been able to remain unchanged from one year to another. Only if the trade unions set out directly and obviously to use their power directly to shape that dynamic pattern have they a lasting hope of influencing its shape and direction. Even a body like the Federal Trade Commission, to which Congress entrusted the enforcement of fair rules of competition, has been described by the TNEC as an instrument by which "monopolistic corporations sought to deprive individual sellers of their freedom to determine their output or prices at which they might sell, or to exclude forces from the industry." [13] Few things are more illuminating as an index to its habits than the activities of the Association of Life Insurance Presidents, which spent nearly half a million dollars annually to lobby against legislation intended to protect the public from principles which would have compelled them to set their house in order. It makes it no better that its objective is announced as the "promotion of sound underwriting practices to prevent abuses cropping up in business." On examination, the "abuses" it seeks to prevent resemble pretty closely the ugly habits of the railroads and the oil industry in the Gilded Age. The Federal Trade Commission's purpose seems the means of safeguarding the great corpora-

[13] Hearings before the Temporary National Economic Committee (Washington), Part 26, pp. 13319-21.

tions from the need to return to the effective structure of genuine competitive enterprise.

The truth, I suggest, is the simple one that the indirect participation of trade unions in politics rests upon the belief that the American economy is still based upon competitive enterprise and that political parties ought not to be the expression of any philosophy which contradicts that belief. Since a party built around a trade-union basis turns rapidly in a socialist direction, it denies the validity of competition, which has been, in a remarkable fashion, rationalized into an expression of the "American way of life." All good Americans are expected to believe in it; even those most aware of the degree to which competition has increasingly given way to combination are expected to announce their conviction that a return to competition is the surest way of remedying all the ills of the American system on its economic side; even the representatives of the steel industry told the Temporary National Economic Committee how hard it was "to visualize in the steel industry how there could be more competition on price without ruining the industry." [14] There could hardly be a better illustration of the degree to which the myth of competitive enterprise as not merely desirable, but also possible, still shapes the character of the American tradition. With this myth, also, there goes the conviction that the government ought to be the vital factor in maintaining the conditions of fair competition, and that it could not do so if the political parties which run the government were tightly fastened to one of the major interest groups in the United States, and this the less since labor in the economic sphere fights to prevent competition between workers and to replace it by combination. Bound up with all this is the sense, so deep in most Americans, that "the party" really means the

[14] *Ibid.*, Part 19, p. 10525.

machine, that the machine means the boss and his assistants, and that they mean the graft and corruption which, especially since the Civil War, have made the word "politician" one of evil repute among so large a proportion of Americans. Few men remember that nearly all the qualities they attribute to a political party belong also to the pressure groups, religious, capitalist, labor-radical; and that these have much the same inner organizational conflicts within themselves as do the Republican and Democratic parties. If they did, they would be far more likely to see that the absence of any general and persistent body of principles in the major political parties makes them little more than arbiters between pressure groups, but arbiters who have the governmental power to satisfy those groups which have done most to enable them to retain *de facto* authority at some particular time. When the business groups bring Mr. McKinley to the White House they expect him to protect them against the evil potentialities of Bryanism. When PAC makes its great contribution to the second and third victories of Franklin Roosevelt, it assumes that he will use all his influence to protect the trade unions and their objectives from defeat by the organized forces of business.

If it is better that the values which are in conflict in politics should be plainly intelligible to the citizen, and organized in terms of intelligibility, it is surely clear that the conflict should take place on a plane where men and women know what they are really deciding. The weakness of the present American system is that most citizens have no such knowledge. They do not know what really lies behind the candidatures of Mr. Landon, or Mr. Willkie, or Mr. Dewey for the presidency, the bargains they have struck, the interests they have privately agreed to placate. The American party system tends to make for irresponsible government; it

hides the real issues beneath the glittering phrases of the
election platforms, trusting that these may, somehow, be
corrected in the tug of war between Congress and its committees, the executive, the Supreme Court. They forget that
the outcome of this tug of war accretes around victories
which become themselves the parents of vested interests
which largely determine the attitude of the defeated power.
Mr. Landon spoke with much vigor against the New Deal.
Mr. Willkie's approach to the electors was notably nearer to
that of Mr. Roosevelt than the approach of his predecessor.
When Mr. Dewey ran against Mr. Roosevelt in 1944, his
speeches read like nothing so much as those of an economic
royalist who had passed through a painful conversion to the
acceptance of the New Deal policies which he hoped to ad-
minister more efficiently than his rival. And when Mr.
Dewey ran against Mr. Truman in 1948, it was hard to say
much more of his speeches than that they were built upon
the principle of maximum inoffensiveness. He would be fair
to labor without being unjust to capital. He was in favor of
progress but anxious to maintain stability. He was for the
greatest possible free trade, though he would not for one
moment interfere with the principles of the American tariff.
He said that there were good things and bad things in the
Taft-Hartley Act. He wanted lower rates of taxation, yet he
favored all those goods, like low-cost housing, which are
rarely compatible with lower taxation. He was for a full
policy of American internationalism so long as it did not
jeopardize Americans' safety from war. In other words, he
offered an eloquently confused picture of hopes and dreams
to the mass of American electorate amid which, had he won,
his promises would have meant little or nothing. Only after
he had entered the White House would the American people
have become aware what exactly were the forces which put

him there, and to which he must seek to pay his debts. That
is why the entrance of the trade unions into politics would
clarify so much that was previously confused. It would make
the choice of the voter a real choice. It would make the
division between parties a real division. It would do more
for the political education of the ordinary trade-union member than even Franklin Roosevelt was able to do. It was far
from the least of his achievements that he made them interested spectators of the political scene; a political party built
around the trade unions would make great numbers of them,
at every level, pass from the role of spectator to the role of
actor. That transition is an urgent need. One of the profoundest weaknesses in American politics is the abstention
of huge numbers of citizens from any political activity; in
1948 only fifty-two per cent of the voters even went to the
polls. At least two-thirds of the American public have expressed their distaste at the idea of their children embarking
upon a political career. About two-thirds of the membership
of both houses of Congress are lawyers, and if the Southern
states are looked at separately, in the two Houses over
seventy-five per cent of the members are lawyers. If one
examines the make-up of a city machine, the Republican
machine in Philadelphia, for instance, one finds some twenty-
seven hundred ward-heelers at its base, each with a small
vested interest in the patronage that comes from victory, but
with no interest in the ideals for which victory is won. And
if one looks at the important figures in the machine, Mr.
Hague in New Jersey, or Mr. Farley when he was the main
organizer of the National Democratic machine, one finds
again that their interest centers on winning votes. There
have been other cases where by the principle of being all
things to all men, and by a use of organized power that
made the brutal merely normal, great party victories have

been won. The skillful combination of personal relations and the right to use the patronage widely enough to fill the party's coffers, to keep the party workers loyal, and to see that the results of "honest graft" went to the right people, and not to the wrong people—these have been the main objects of party organization.

The United States covers such a large area that the building of a new party could not help being a far more difficult task than it has been in European countries. Sectional interests are an obstacle to unified action. Religious differences have a thicker political nature than they have in mainly Protestant democracies like Great Britain or the Scandinavian countries or New Zealand. Inherited national differences go deeper the more heterogeneous the origins of the populations. Yet, granted all this, the matters on which the American trade unions have now got to make up their minds go far beyond their national problems and their relations with their employers; and they involve issues far more constant than any which can be handled by auctioning their support at each election to the highest bidder. It ought to be obvious by now that President Roosevelt's hope of getting a permanent alliance between the government on the one side, and the trade unions and employers' organizations on the other, was a temporary expedient only. It worked up to the outbreak of the Second World War only because he had, as the great depression involved him in a vast emergency program, to keep the support of the trade unions. Once confidence had been restored, he could not regain the sympathy of business leaders until the war dragged the United States into a position where there were both full employment and a crisis that transcended most economic differences between capital and labor. The congressional elections of 1946 showed how much the trade-union electorate was still confused over the issues,

even the domestic issues, it faced; and the number of unions
is small which seek by educational effort to prepare their
members to transcend this confusion. Anyone who reads
President Roosevelt's speech of March 23, 1935, with its un-
answerable denunciation of the backward social conditions
in the South, the grimly low wages earned there, the reactionary habits of Southern landlords, must bear in mind that
none of these has yet been dealt with in the four years since
the end of the Second World War; and that the filibuster
in the Senate of February-March 1949 is, above all, an attempt by President Truman's own party to prevent Congress
from dealing with the problems of the South, especially with
lynching and that economic backwardness which is so
largely the result of the employer's exploitation of "poor
white" labor in return for an unstated agreement that the
Negroes in the South shall retain a permanently inferior
status in all aspects of the national life. It is difficult enough
for the trade unions to maintain full employment at high
wages and short hours in any permanent way if the purchasing power of the South cannot be mobilized to secure a
greater use of American productive power. It would be
still more difficult if the gap between production and consumption could not be bridged by methods like the European Recovery Program and the overwhelming expenditure
on armaments, both of which have a public works aspect as
well as an international aspect.

The trade unions have now to think about problems with
which the leaders of Mr. Gompers' day had hardly to concern themselves. Their own future is bound up with decisions on European recovery, the road taken by the Asiatic
powers in the next generation, and with the success of the
effort President Truman has waged to modernize the economic organization of the backward areas of the world. In

that effort, on a short-term view, he will not find it easy to win the support of some, at least, of the great corporations. It is at least open to doubt whether a Middle East in which the present feudalism is broken will suit the oil interests as well as one in which it is maintained. A predominantly Communist China, if it insists on retaining the ownership of its national resources, will not be as obvious a source of investment for the great financial corporations as in the past. Every attempt to rescue Central and South American communities from actual poverty and spasmodic attacks of mean dictatorships will not win an eager welcome from some of the most powerful investment banks in the United States. There can be no doubt that the policy of economic modernization is, from its inception, an important way of strengthening American trade unions, if only because the process will call for immense aid from American technicians and a constant flow of American capital goods. But the trade unions must learn that this is the case and mobilize all their power to see that such a program is not delayed by those who know that its results will affect the power of the great business interests to hold whole countries to ransom, as the Patino family, for example, are able from their New York domicile to control the life of Bolivia. Economic modernization in the backward areas means freedom; and freedom established abroad safeguards freedom in the United States itself. Every blow at freedom abroad is a blow at the security of the American trade unions.

To this I venture to add a brief note on the most delicate of all contemporary issues. Most American trade unions are anti-Russian, and support with little hesitation the "cold war" the government of the United States is waging. Most of them are also strongly anti-communistic; and many trade-union leaders, both in the CIO and the AFL, have fought

with all their energy to drive Communist officials out of the
unions and to support attacks upon them in fields quite remote from trade-union concern. On the latter policy I hazard
the guess that any large-scale witch-hunting merely clears
the ground of one symbol of evil so that the business leaders
can move, step by step, to the position where they can again
seek to bring the trade-union leader once more to the attention of the public as a symbol of evil; it is always dangerous
to create a class of citizens in a democracy as a scapegoat for
public indignation. It may go far to split a trade-union movement, which is already in urgent need of unity, to a point
where it loses the power to stand up to aggressive attack,
which has been its chief gain since 1933.

It is easy to find strong reasons for both indignation and
sorrow at the line Soviet Russia has taken since 1945. But it
is a far harder, and more important, task for the trade unions
to realize how easily a "cold war" may turn into a "hot war."
If we all became involved in that third world war which
could swiftly emerge from the present situation, at its end,
even if the anti-Russian forces were victorious—a matter
upon which some skepticism is permissible—I do not think
it would be possible, in the light of the material and spiritual
devastation it would involve, to maintain that special combination of capitalism and democracy of which the United
States is now the supreme example. And, granted its present
social structure, the democracy is far more likely to disappear than the capitalism. To safeguard the latter, the
major need of the business leaders will be to break the
strength of the trade unions. It is these, therefore, which
have a greater interest than any other institution of American democracy to end the danger of war. But as a pressure
group they have neither the organic relation to the federal
government, nor the power to act with the necessary swift-

ness over a wide front, that will become increasingly essential if the "cold war" continues. They could not fight it in the workshops or the ports without massive strikes of an ominous character; they could fight it only on the political front. But on this front a pressure group must recognize that its strength is far less in international matters than it is on issues of domestic concern. The danger it can scarcely hope to avoid is that, fighting a world war through the institutions of capitalist democracy, it may find itself compelled to support what will be regarded as no more than the temporary suspension of democracy for its duration, only to discover that, at its close, the security of capitalism is assured while the restoration of democracy is a profoundly difficult matter even after victory, and probably impossible after defeat. The trade unions, in fact, must be very careful lest the alliance with business and government into which they have been led by their natural dislike of communist totalitarianism does not make them the unconscious instruments of a counter-revolution which addresses them in the name of freedom. The Taft-Hartley Act was passed to protect the freedom of the American workingman; and the leader of the Conservative party in Great Britain has promised that if the Labour government is defeated at the next general election he will free the British workingman. If you inquire from what fetters he is to be released, the answer is that it is from the obligations he assumes as a trade-union member. It is not an exaggeration to say that the worker who is freed from his trade union is thereby left in servitude to his employer.

I may, perhaps, add here one other remark. I am not urging the desirability of an American labor party built around the trade unions merely because that has been the course of British trade-union development. But I do not accept the view that the social-economic situation in the United States is so unique that its evolution will be special to itself. On the contrary, I think the same causes are discernible in the operation of the American system as there have been in Great Britain; and they are not less likely to produce the same effect. Without the ability to express their purposes in a direct political way, American trade unions will remain unable to mobilize their full political power. Only a continual emergency has enabled the trade unions to go forward as they have done in the last sixteen years. If it became either much more, or much less, intense, I doubt whether the recent progress would continue. Neither of the historic parties is interested in the trade unions except in relation to its own hold upon the governments, both in the states and in the federal sphere; the real ally of the Republican party is the corporation, and the Democratic party depends upon the South, the machines in the big cities, and, in an important degree, the Roman Catholic Church. It requires quite special circumstances to make an alliance between the trade unions and these parties; and the goodwill would inevitably be interstitial. That is why I think that trade unions should express their aspirations through an independent political party of their own and make that the center about which are aggregated all the vital forces of progressivism in America. I do not profess to see how this party will be made nor for what precise objectives it will search; and I am sure that it will be an American labor party deriving all that matters most in its ethos from the American scene. But it is only when it has come into effective being that the American labor movement will fully play the role that is naturally fitted to its character in a great industrial society. It cannot begin to play that role too soon.

III. TRADE UNIONS
AND THE LAW

1

I CANNOT here even attempt to touch upon the vast and innumerable issues that arise in the courts out of the relation between the trade unions and the community. I must limit myself to the discussion of one principle of the Common Law and examine it in a few only of its many aspects. That principle is the effort of the courts, ever since the seventeenth century, to promote freedom of trade, and thus to regard all limits upon freedom of contract with a growing malevolence. The Common Law has been one of the major historical instruments of the market economy, the ardent protector of the maximum possible competition; and its place in the development of the market economy has been so important that it is not a serious exaggeration to say that it has hardly less created the market economy than been the outcome of its triumph about the middle of the nineteenth century. We can trace, almost step by step, the conscious effort of the judges, especially after the Revolution of 1688, to adapt the Common Law to new commercial needs. It is of high importance to recognize that the statesmen who invited William and Mary to occupy the English throne, upon the convenient, if fictitious, assumption that James II had abdicated, drew their main support from the mercantile class; and that the members of this class not only urgently desired the removal of all restrictions upon freedom of trade, but were unceasingly, through their power in the House of

Commons, working to secure it. We can see the courts at
work adapting the law of contract to the demands of the
merchants. The technique was superbly displayed by Lord
Macclesfield (Chief Justice Parker) in 1733 in the classic
case of *Mitchel* v. *Reynolds*.[1] This is, I think, the point at
which it becomes decisively clear that the Common Law will
be so interpreted that it opens out those channels of opportunity so essential to the market economy, and so fatal to the
medieval idea that the test of valid law is justice.

Lord Macclesfield spoke in accents which the Supreme
Court of the United States would have completely understood in the years following the Civil War. He did not doubt
that there must be restraints upon freedom of trade. The
real problem was to be assured that the restraints imposed
were reasonable. What therefore matters is the criteria by
which we test whether or not a restraint is a reasonable one.
It must not be a restraint that prevents a man from earning
his living. It should not be a restraint that works to the
detriment of the community by preventing it from enjoying
the capacity of one of its citizens. It should not disadvantage
the apprentice by restraining him from setting up for himself
once he has served his articles. Not least, no restraint should
be admitted to protect those corporations which labor for
exclusive advantages in trade and reduce them to as few
hands as possible. And it is of the highest interest to note
that in two famous cases, in 1894,[2] and in 1916,[3] respectively,
the courts in a very different economic atmosphere broadly
restated Lord Macclesfield's case for one trade with appropriate but small adaptations. To this must be added the
significant fact that it was after the Revolution of 1688, also,

[1] P. Wms. 183.
[2] *Nordenfeldt* v. *The Maxim Nordenfeldt*, A.C. 535 (1894).
[3] *Harris* v. *Saxelby*, A.C. 688 (1916).

that the law of employers' liability was given its modern form by the courts, and especially by Chief Justice Holt. The growth of vicarious liability he made possible was obviously needed to facilitate the general, and especially the corporate, expansion in enterprise. In 1685 it was the law that the master was responsible for his servants' torts only if he gave his servants special authority for acts that had tortious results.[4] By 1691 Holt was arguing that "whoever employs another is answerable for him, and undertakes for his care to all that make use of him "[5] What is really fascinating about the doctrine of employers' liability is that in an age of swift commercial growth Holt should at once have seen the necessity for imposing it on a Common Law which had seen no validity in it for five hundred years, and that he should have made it the basis of the doctrine of public policy.[6] It is only less fascinating than the fact that the doctrine of vicarious liability should exclude a fellow-servant from its scope in England until 1880, nearly two hundred years; and that it should take yet another sixteen years before Parliament, not without considerable pain to the judges, should insist upon the acceptance of the principle of workmen's compensation.

You will note that at a time when the economic system was moving from the idea of regulation to the idea of laissez faire, and moving there in an age of rapid commercial expansion, the judges—not least significantly, the great judges—were preparing to adapt the principles of the Common Law to what the changing economic system would require. There was to be free competition, the open market, whenever they seemed "reasonable," whenever they were not contrary to "public policy." The desirability of free competition reached

---

[4] *Kingston* v. *Booth*, Skinner 228.

[5] *Boson* v. *Sandford*, 2 Salkeld 440.

[6] *Hern* v. *Nichols*, 1 Salkeld 239 (1709).

its zenith in the English courts in the famous Mogul
Steamship case in 1892.[7] Here the doctrine of free competition resulted in two findings. The first was that a combination of capital may completely dominate an industry without becoming a conspiracy in restraint of trade; that it is
perfectly proper either for persons or for corporations to join
together to prevent a newcomer to an industry threatening
their hold upon it; that there is no illegality in size, as there
is no illegality in the merciless use of power. The second was
that a corporation holding the immense position of the defendant corporation in the Mogul Steamship case may
legally say to third parties, such as merchants who want to
ship goods, that it will not take their goods to any area
where the vessels go, unless the merchants agree not to deal
with any other shipping line in that area but the defendant
corporation. Free competition, in other words, was, as a
matter of public policy, so desirable that when translated
into the Common Law it gave a monopoly intended to suppress competition the privilege of legal protection, a privilege that included the right to impose the secondary boycott
upon interests not concerned with the original dispute. Nor
was this twofold doctrine called into question in England until, in 1948, Parliament gave the Board of Trade the
power to set up a Monopolies Commission which would inquire into restrictive practices such as the Mogul case revealed. If the Commission finds such practices proved, the
President of the Board of Trade may, subject to the consent
of Parliament, take steps to prevent their operation. As the
first cases were to be heard by the Commission only in
March 1949, it is obviously too early to say what results its
work is likely to have. There are people in politics, both on

[7] *Mogul Steamship Company* v. *McGregor, Gaw & Company*, A.C. 25
(1892).

the Right and on the Left, who look to the new machinery with immense hope, confident that it will break up price-rings and the like. For myself, looking at the outcome of the Sherman Act, I am not yet disposed to believe that genuinely free competition will replace the natural evolution of the combination which always follows when competition is strong, until we have seen the new system in operation. Few things have been as wisely said as Adam Smith's famous remark that "people of the same trade seldom meet together, even for merriment or decision, but the conversation ends in a conspiracy against the public, or a contrivance to raise prices." [8]

It is impossible to survey this development without comparing the attitude of the courts to the workers and their combinations for natural protection—the trade unions. I cannot hope to trace here the difference in the adaptation of the doctrines of the Common Law to the employers on the one hand, and to the workers on the other. It is not merely that until the Trade Union Law Amendment Acts of 1874–75 a trade union was always liable to be caught in the meshes of conspiracy. It is not merely, either, that, while the Combination Acts of 1799–1800 had a profound influence upon the workers, no case is known in which any employers were indicted under its provisions, nor even paid any attention to them. Far more revealing is what happened when, after the decision in the Mogul case, the trade unions assumed that they also could promote the welfare of their members by similar methods to those of the shipowners, provided that their behavior was not tortious or criminal. *Allen* v. *Flood* [9] in 1898 and *Quinn* v. *Leathem* [10] in 1901

---

[8] Adam Smith, *Wealth of Nations* (New York: The Modern Library, 1937), p. 130.
[9] *Allen* v. *Flood*, A.C. 1 (1898).
[10] *Quinn* v. *Leathem*, A.C. 495 (1901).

both illustrate quite admirably how unwise it is for any trade union to assume that the law applies to them in the same way as it applies to their masters. It is, of course, true that in *Allen* v. *Flood* the trade union was successful in the House of Lords by six against three. But in his minority opinion Lord Halsbury, the Lord Chancellor, not only said that every man has the right to get work and keep at work without any interference from others; he inferred that right from what he called "that freedom from restraint, that liberty of action . . . found running through the principles of our law." That is to say, that a trade union, in his view, could not interfere with freedom of contract by using its power to get jobs for its members, though a great shipping corporation was permitted to use its power to drive a competitor out of business. It is easy to understand why Lord Herschell, in the majority opinion, not only said that trade unionists, as long as they do not break the law, "are entitled to further their interests in the manner which seems to them best, and most likely to be effectual," but remarked also, no doubt with the Mogul case in mind, that competition was not "regarded with special favor by the law," nor, in his belief, "should be so regarded." *Allen* v. *Flood* was, on the surface, a victory for the trade union; but it showed that the criteria of "reasonableness" and "public policy" might easily vary with the composition of the court of last instance which applied these criteria in any particular case.

Three years later, in *Quinn* v. *Leathem,* an Irish case where the trade union sought the right to make a wholesale butcher give its members preference in the employment of his workers, and used its power to win this right, just as the shipowners had done, by insisting that his largest customer should refrain from dealing with him unless he complied with the union's demand, it found that, as far as trade

unions were concerned, the secondary boycott was illegal.
The House of Lords confirmed the decision of the Irish
courts, and the propositions laid down by a very able judge,
Lord Brampton, on the majority side, are of extraordinary
interest. He relied upon two principles: a trade union was
different from a business corporation in that it could not use
its power "as legitimate trade competition"; and by applying
the secondary boycott, just as in the Mogul case, it was engaged in an illegal conspiracy to cause damage to Leathem,
since it was not seeking "to obtain or maintain fair hours of
labour at fair wages, or to promote a good understanding between employers and employed, and workman and workman, or for the settlement of any disputes, for none had
existence." These two principles, Brampton thought, distinguished the use of a trade union's power from the use of a
business corporation's power. Its effort to protect its members from unemployment was, somehow, different in kind
from the effort of a combination of shipowners to protect
their market against competition. Therefore a trade union
which brought indirect pressure to bear upon one employer
to influence another was guilty of conspiracy, while a shipping corporation which brought indirect pressure to bear on
a rival was not guilty of conspiracy. Employers would use
the most ruthless form of competition to crush a rival so
long as they did this for self-advancement and in the pursuit
of gain. But, in some mysterious way, parallel action by
trade unions was illegal, even though the layman might
think that the more strongly an industry was unionized, the
higher would be likely to be the wages of its members—
which, surely, is the pursuit of gain—while the better the
conditions obtained by the union, the more likely would it
be to attract workers to membership—which may surely be
described, without unfairness, as self-advancement. And

Brampton was stoutly supported by Lord Halsbury, Lord Chancellor still in 1901, when he said that if, on behalf of his union, Quinn could do what he had sought to do against Leathem, "it could hardly be said that our jurisprudence was that of a civilized community."

You can see that these cases involved enormous issues. The House of Lords, in the Mogul case, said that the Common Law, aiming at the establishment of the fullest possible competition, could give its blessing to a corporation which left no stone unturned in its determined effort to establish a monopoly in its field. Here, indeed, is a court of law legislating on the grand scale in the area of social policy that most of us would naturally assign to elected members of a legislature rather than to a chance majority of appointed judges, some of whom we know to have been chosen as much on political as on legal grounds. The principle becomes still more striking when, after its period of indecision in *Allen* v. *Flood*, the House of Lords said flatly that trade unionism had no resemblance to business enterprise, in the usual sense of that term, when it tried to protect itself by means it was told were legal when practiced by employers. Any sensible trade-union member would be bound to look at this extraordinary result and conclude that if there is not one law for the rich and another for the poor—which cannot, of course, be the case since we all enjoy the equal protection of the laws—it is very difficult to understand how there can be one law for trade unions and a quite different, and far more advantageous, law for employers and their associations. He would be tempted to conclude that the decision to look at the two areas of action as though they bore no resemblance to one another ought to be a quite deliberate decision of a legislative assembly, and that those who arrive at this conclusion could reasonably be asked to justify their view

when they stood as candidates at the next general election.
He might be so tempted; but he would have to resist the
temptation since the only way to overturn the decision of
the Law Lords in Great Britain is to persuade the government to reverse their view, or to amend it by Act of Parliament. That is more easily said than done. It took five years
and the successful formation of a new party in the House of
Commons to reverse the notorious decision in the Taff Vale
case; and it took almost twenty years to reverse the vindictive Trade Union Law Amendment of 1927, the authority
for which was largely built on a remark of Mr. Justice Ast-
bury, which was quite irrelevant to the granting of the injunction for which he was asked, and on the legal reputation
of Sir John Simon, who told Parliament and the country
what it is now safe to say was wholly inaccurate, that a
general strike in pursuance of a trade dispute is both unconstitutional and illegal.

I have not one atom of doubt that the eminent judges who
decided these cases arrived at their conclusions not only
after full discussion among themselves, but with a really
genuine desire to be detached from bias on either side. They
have not, however, persuaded everyone to accept their outlook. Lord Citrine, now Chairman of the Nationalized Electricity Authority, but until 1945 the General Secretary of
the Trades Union Congress—and no one will accuse Lord
Citrine of a natural distrust of established institutions of
Great Britain—said that "with the experience of the past . . .
the trade-union movement has little faith in either the competence or the impartiality of the courts in matters affecting
organized labor"; [11] and, were it necessary, I could cite great
scholars, a former Attorney-General, and even Mr. Winston

[11] *The Times of London,* May 7, 1927.

Churchill, in support of that view.[12] I am not even sure that Lord Citrine's statement, made under circumstances which were not privileged, was not guilty of being an illegal utterance in that his words were calculated to bring the established institutions of his country, or, at any rate, the judiciary, within the range of the Blasphemous and Seditious Libel Act of 1819. I cannot but remind you of the well-known words of Mr. Justice Miller upon the factors which moved some of his colleagues to the choice of their *rationes decidendo*.[13] Nor can I avoid insisting upon the overwhelming importance of President Roosevelt's remark that "every time they [the judges] interpret contract, property, vested interests, due process, liberty, they necessarily enact into the law parts of a system of social philosophy. . . . The decisions of the courts upon economic and social questions depend on their economic and social philosophy; and for the peaceful progress of our people during the twentieth century we shall owe most to those judges who hold to a twentieth-century social philosophy, and not to a long-outgrown philosophy, which was then the product of primitive economic conditions." [14]

I need hardly attempt to show that the habits of the British courts are pretty well on all fours with the habits of American courts. This is, of course, the case. The decisions to which I have referred are merely illustrations of a general rule that the tendency, in courts where the historic principles of the Common Law are accepted, is to put corporations in a category where they can be judged by criteria quite different from those by which a trade union is judged. I do not, of

[12] See my *Parliamentary Government in England* (New York: Viking Press, 1938).

[13] Charles Fairman, *Mr. Justice Miller and the Supreme Court* (Cambridge: Harvard University Press, 1939), *passim*.

[14] *Congressional Record*, Part 1, p. 21 (1943).

course, mean that there are no exceptions to this rule. As long
ago as 1896 Mr. Justice Holmes, in a famous Massachusetts
dissent,[15] was able to see that the creation of these different
criteria was indefensible. He is only the most outstanding judge who was able to rise above his own private universe of conviction—but he is still one in a minority. Most
judges have not doubted that large aggregations of capital
have rights which must be protected against the claims of
large aggregations of men. The doctrine of public policy has
been invoked in a good many ways to put the rights of
property above human welfare. Judges who have insisted
that rates must be so fixed for some public utility as to secure a return upon the capital invested that is not "con-
fiscatory" in character have equally insisted that the establishment of a minimum wage, or the limitation of the hours
of labor, or the prohibition of child labor by federal action,
are all of them unconstitutional. Few things are more amazing than the eulogy bestowed on the Cleveland government
by Mr. Justice Brewer in the Debs case. "It is more to the
praise than to the blame of the government," he wrote,
"that, instead of determining for itself questions of right and
wrong on the part of these petitioners and their associates,
and enforcing that determination by the club of the police-
man and the bayonet of the soldier, it submitted all these
questions to the peaceful determination of judicial tribu-
nals." [16] After the decisive examination of the use of the injunction in industrial disputes by Frankfurter and Greene,[17]
I do not want to say more than that, when it came, the
Norris-La Guardia Act had been long overdue.

[15] *Vegelahn* v. *Guntner.*
[16] *In re Debs,* 158 U.S. 564.
[17] Felix Frankfurter and Nathan Greene, *The Labor Injunction* (New
York: Macmillan, 1930).

Anyone who compares the status of trade unions before the law when the Combination Acts were passed one hundred and fifty years ago by Parliament, with their status today, both in the United States and Great Britain, cannot but admit a great advance. But there is, to be frank, always a shadow looming over that advance, and no one can ever be certain when it is going to fall. It is not easy, but it is nevertheless important, to try to explain the nature of this shadow. To do so, I must go back to the attitude of the governing class of Great Britain to combinations of workmen from, roughly, the outbreak of the French Revolution to the repeal of the Combination Acts in 1824–25. It is clear that Pitt and his colleagues fought combinations of workmen because they were afraid that they might become vehicles for the conveyance of the evil ideas which had resulted in the tragic events in France. To make the swift punishment of trade unions possible was to stop the danger of political agitation, to preserve the peace, and to safeguard prosperity. The government feared that events in France might be imitated in England. Their informants, peers of the realm, soldiers, justices of the peace, and the clergy, as well as businessmen themselves, usually regarded a strike as the necessary prelude to disorder and were disturbed by what the Deputy Adjutant-General, Colonel de Lancy, on a tour of inspection in 1792, called "the unreasonable demands of the populace." [18] Colonel de Lancy argued that trade unions "must very materially hurt the trade of the place by enabling other countries to undersell them." [19] The Home Secretary sent frequent circulars of advice to the magistrates on how to suppress the conspiracies of workmen. In 1818 Henry Hob-

[18] Arthur Aspinall (ed.), *The Early English Trade Unions* (London: Batchworth, 1949), p. 5; an invaluable collection of hitherto unpublished documents.
[19] *Ibid.*

house, then Undersecretary of State for Home Affairs, wrote at length to the Chief Justice of Chester expressing his fear that "the system of combination . . . extends not merely to a conspiracy in each trade of the journeymen against their masters, but a scheme is actually in progress for forming a combination in all trades to afford reciprocal aid to each other." [20] Hobhouse expressed his fear lest the "timidity of the masters" prevent the Chief Justice from having men before him on indictment for conspiracy; but he begged him to make "a luminous exposition of the law on that subject . . . and if you should feel it right to add a word or two on the duty of detecting and counteracting such conspiracies, they would be well applied to the existing circumstances." In 1818 a Lancashire correspondent informed Hobhouse that "their discontents are secretly fomented by that spirit which has so long disturbed the quiet of the country, and which would urge them on to violence if an opportunity should present itself for making an impression." [21] Lord Sidmouth, then Home Secretary, wrote in deep regret that the weavers should have been brought to a concession "no less decisive in its probable consequences than dangerous in its immediate example." He admitted the possibility that the workers' claims might originally have been reasonable, but he regretted that they should have been admitted "when those by whom they were preferred were engaged in an unlawful combination to enforce them." [22]

What was felt by the laboring class, and by the government, was felt with equal intensity by the justices of the peace and by the judges. "I am convinced from what I see and hear in every direction that the lower classes are radi-

[20] *Ibid.*, pp. 277-78.
[21] *Ibid.*, p. 279.
[22] *Ibid.*, pp. 282-83.

cally corrupted," wrote a clerical justice of the peace to Sidmouth in 1818. "An advance of wages or prices for work done, as I have before intimated, is a mere stalking horse. . . . Their aim is revolution." What the government and its correspondents feared was hardly less feared by the judges of the High Court; and it is only necessary to examine decisions like those of Mr. Justice Williams in the classic case of the Dorchester Labourers, as late as 1834, to realize how long and how intense was the panic it caused. The simple fact is that, generally, the professional and manufacturing classes joined with the government, as Mr. and Mrs. Hammond have so brilliantly shown; [23] and that, at least until some such time as 1848, the government and the courts played into each other's hands in order to destroy the attractions of trade unionism. These groups became committed to the idea that the courts must be used to smash a nascent radicalism, which magistrate after magistrate was convinced, in the words of one of them, was the outcome of "the machinations of demagogues and disappointed reformers." If the distressed workers, he thought, could only be separated from such influences, they would be found "extremely well behaved, and always thankful for a very moderate pittance of parochial relief." [24]

2

All this English history is a hundred and fifty years old. Anyone who reads it all in detail, and examines, in relation to it, the treatment meted out to the trade unions and their

[23] J. L. L. and B. Hammond, *The Town Labourer, 1760–1832* (New York: Longmans, Green, 1917); *The Skilled Labourer, 1760–1832* (New York: Longmans, Green, 1919); *The Village Labourer, 1760–1832* (New York: Longmans, Green, 1920).

[24] Aspinall, *op. cit.*, p. 273. This is dated August 17, 1818.

members, will be wise to remember that the history of a century and a half ago might only too easily become the framework for a similar history tomorrow. I venture to doubt, for example, whether the authors of the Norris-La Guardia Act assumed that their legislation would not apply to any industry which, by reason of its importance, the President might take over under the threat of a strike in it. I am, first of all, discouraged by the tortured construction by which the court reached this result. To say that the Act does not apply to the government in its capacity as employer because Congress does not especially mention this, and because, during the discussions of the measure in Congress, this was not brought out as one of the reasons for its passage, is dangerously akin in character to Mr. Justice Farwell's decision in the Taff Vale case. If Mr. Chief Justice Vinson is right, whenever the President decides to take over an industry those employed in it come under the power the injunction implies. Obviously this raises two further questions. The first is whether the judges are bound to accept the President's view that an emergency exists or whether they may themselves pass upon the issue of whether the President is right or wrong. If they think the power is solely in the President's hands, we are obviously back at the situation which sent Debs to prison over the Pullman strike under Cleveland. Anyone who analyzes the details of the method used to move Cleveland to action can easily see how a weak President could be persuaded or coerced or even tricked into taking possession on emergency grounds. If, on the other hand, an emergency is what, in final analysis, the Supreme Court says it is, who can doubt that a difference of opinion between the executive and the judiciary on a matter of this importance may easily work irreparable damage to both?

Nor does the problem end here. If the President takes

over the railroads or the mines, it is because a dispute has occurred between the owners and the trade unions. To prevent that dispute ending in a strike, the President makes himself what is in fact a fictitious owner of an industry in which nothing else changes. The same managers remain; the same foremen remain. The only change is that the trade unions are legally bound not to strike under penalty of an injunction. If they ignore the injunction, the penalties imposed by the court might easily do such damage to the union as to make the employers the autocrats of industry much in the way that the steel barons and Mr. Henry Ford insisted on acting like autocrats until the combination of the Norris-La Guardia Act and the Wagner Act cut the ground from under their feet. I do not need to draw upon the hatred felt by the most backward of trade unions against the use of the injunction. To keep it as a weapon which government may use is, I suggest, to insure two things. It will make the unions once more bitter against the government and bitter against the courts. The only people who stand to gain from it are the employers. Once they can persuade the President to go through the fiction of taking them over, they know that the law will be invoked to prevent the dislocation of the empires they own. I find it difficult to believe, despite the fact that Mr. Lewis sent his miners back to the pits, that he, or they, will always act that way. I think it still more difficult to believe that a President will always find trade unions as pliant as the two railway brotherhoods were in 1946. And anyone who examines closely the powers the President asked from Congress in the threatened railway strike will conclude, if he is capable of detachment, that there was not a scintilla of democracy in his proposals. He was asking for compulsory labor to replace free trade unions. He was asking for criminal penalties against any trade-union leader who helps to run a strike or fails to take action to end it. A President asks for powers to draft the workers in such an industry into the Army, where, of course, refusal to obey orders becomes at once mutiny, with all its rigorous penalties. Just at the time, in fact, when these enormous powers are being taken away from industry, the government asks that, in an emergency like the transition from a war economy to a peace economy, it should have the rights that have been taken from the big employers, because they so frequently abused them.

It is really no answer to say that the right to strike will go only in the industries which are vital to American national life. No one would dare to draw up a list of such industries. Some are overwhelmingly clear, like coal, and transport, and shipping. But what of the food industries, and the chemical industries, and the steel industry? What of armament works? What of food distribution? What of banks? What of elevator men in the great skyscrapers? Is it not clear that there is a boundary where deep differences of opinion as to whether some given industry is inside or outside that boundary are wholly justified? And if deep differences are justified, is there substantial ground for leaving its line to be defined by a President whose weak subordination to powerful industrial interests may be his outstanding quality? His credit goes if the Supreme Court turns him down; he establishes a very dangerous precedent if he succeeds. And I venture to think that those who believe that we ought to abolish the right to strike in any vital industry ought to be aware of what they are really doing. The government takes over an industry, thereby throwing all its authority against the strikers; but when a settlement has been reached, the industry goes back to private ownership, which has then the knowledge that, if it refuses to entertain a claim from the trade union, it has a fair certainty that the government will not permit the workers to strike; so that, in fact, it knows that normally the government will settle negotiations on its behalf and that it is highly unlikely that the government is going to keep the industry, in the present climate of American opinion, in its own hands. Of all the dangers this situation presents, only Mr. Justice Rutledge and Mr. Justice Murphy seem to me to have any full sense. We are left, by the majority opinion, with the danger that, once again, as so often in the past, the claims of labor are subordinate to those of corporate power. More than this: in these two dramatic instances the trade unions by thoroughly bad leadership have left the impression that presidential interference has made him the protector of consumer interests; there are at least some millions of Americans who believe that the government acts in the name of the ordinary consumer, that when it protects the employer it is really protecting consumer sovereignty. To my mind this kind of conclusion is fatal to all concerned.

I think this is a wholly mistaken view. The government protects the consumer when it runs an industry in his interest. But it does not run it in his interest if it leaves it in private hands in quiet times but takes it over at once in an emergency. I hope I am not trespassing on ground that a foreigner ought not to occupy if I say that the main motive of those who got the Taft-Hartley Act through was far less concerned with the consumers than with pulling the strongest teeth out of the Wagner Act. What they saw, and when they secured its passage over the President's veto saw pretty clearly, was that labor's power in Congress is only that of one pressure group among many, and that if they did their job efficiently they could make the employers' pressure group appear far more public-spirited in Congress and the newspapers, as well as in the movies and on the radio, than the trade unions could hope to do. I think they were right; for, outside the unions themselves, I cannot find that the Taft-Hartley Act aroused much bitter opposition from the masses. It may have thrown trade-union votes to Mr. Truman at the presidential election; do the figures show that it achieved much more? I think not, for two reasons: first, because few trade unions saw the range of the implications of the Act; and, second, because since the end of the Second World War the trade unions have failed to make that deep impact on non-union America, or union America, for that matter, which they ought to have done. I think that conclusion is implicit in Judge Goldsborough's decision, and he reached it because nothing the unions had done made him realize the significance of the frontiers labor had reached by the time the New Deal was over. He felt that labor was exacting its pound of flesh in an emergency and that his job was to prevent it from doing so. What he found, the amount of the fines he imposed apart, the Supreme Court accepted. What does this mean?

At least, I suggest, three important things. It means, first of all, that the judges follow public opinion, and do not lead it, in taking the view that where economic crisis threatens a community the government, even at the level of city or county, may fairly be regarded as an impartial arbiter between the employers and the employed whose conflict has, in fact, been in some causal relationship with the crisis. The government, for them, is above the battle. Its proposals are not selfish or narrow or one-sided. What it seeks to do is to take action on behalf of the whole community, the interests of which it is seeking to safeguard. It means, second, that there is a kind of residuary estate from the old doctrine of conspiracy, capable at any moment of remarkable expansion, the impact of which is far more likely to prevent the trade union, rather than the employers, from getting justice. It means, third, that the judges have been influenced by the fact that there is a barrier of ill-feeling between the trade unions and the rest of the American people which the trade-union leaders have not yet learned to surmount. I think that was shown by at least two decisive facts. The first was that outside trade-union circles there was no national protest against the Taft-Hartley Act, and that the interests behind its promotion were pretty well aware that they could count upon the absence of that protest. Otherwise, they would never have been able to muster enough votes, even in a Republican Congress, to pass the bill over the President's veto. The second is that both Judge Goldsborough and the majority of the Supreme Court were able to restore government by injunction so easily after the long and bitter fight of fifty years to get rid of it. This is not only significant in itself. It is especially significant because in the next generation the government will enter increasingly into the framework of American industrial life. Whether it enters by way of an extension of public ownership, or whether it enters because, without its aid, there may be a break in economic continuities held by the President to be vital, will make very little difference. The precedent set by the Supreme Court puts the trade unions at a heavy disadvantage in their efforts; and were there to be a malevolently reactionary president, with a Congress of the same temper supporting him, there are wide areas of activity over which trade unions might find that their hard-won freedom is in grave jeopardy.

For it must be remembered that there is a constant, skillful pressure to make the public believe that the trade unions have now got out of hand and lost any sense of proportion or of responsibility. The idea of the closed shop is presented as a monstrous form of tyranny. It interferes with the employer's right to choose his own workmen, and with the workman's right to join or not to join a trade union without coercion from anybody. The strike weapon is presented as the final lever. It is conveniently forgotten that the vast majority of trade-union leaders will recommend any reasonable compromise for acceptance rather than run the risks inherent in any strike of real magnitude. The demand of the trade unions for the right to a better wage when a great corporation, like General Motors, for example, makes large profits is met in two ways: partly by the insistence that if the trade unions want to share in booms they must also share in slumps; and partly by a refusal to open the corporation's books to union inspection. In the second case, General Motors has said, the union is really seeking to encroach upon the sphere of management, and that this encroachment is merely the prelude to a situation when the unions will try to dominate business. They are bitten, it is said, by a lust for power which is equally a threat to property on the one hand, and to the right of the public to pay prices as low as the big corporations can keep them on the other. Even taking Mr. Truman's remarkable victory in the presidential election of 1948 into account, I should venture to guess that the corporations have been pretty successful in getting these views accepted by the general public outside the unions themselves. It is notable how popular has become the view that strikes in essential industries are increasingly an abuse of power. It is still more notable that President Truman won very considerable applause when in the spring of 1946 he broke a possible railway strike by methods that most of the modern dictators would not have disdained to use. A public that is tired of seeing an increasing cost of living and of the fear that some big industrial stoppage may cost many thousands of men quite outside the area of dispute their jobs begins to say that the unions are really getting out of hand.

You will not forget the resentment provoked by the influence Mr. Hillman exercised with Mr. Roosevelt; and, not least, the indignation at his successful use of PAC. I do not think I am wrong in saying that when Judge Goldsborough imposed those heavy penalties upon Mr. John L. Lewis for contempt there was a glow of satisfaction which had its echoes inside large areas of the trade-union movement as well as outside it. That glow put the trade unions on the defensive. It raised, for many, the question of whether the gains labor made in the New Deal period were not excessive. It made the initiative in action pass from the frontier defined in the great period of President Roosevelt's progressive ascendancy to a different frontier where the initiative lay somewhere between the White House and the Capitol. And it is worth noting that, though in November 1948 President Truman pledged himself to repeal the Taft-Hartley Act, it is by no means certain that his congressional majority will give him the simple and direct repeal for which he campaigned. A revised version of that repeal may push the frontier a good deal more over to the employers' side than anything one could have predicted before 1938. I should like to be sure that this change in the frontier boundaries has been fully and clearly understood by the fifteen million trade unionists in the United States today.

You may ask why I emphasize these points in a discussion of the trade unions and the courts. I do so because the mind of the public is a mind by which judges have been deeply, though very often unconsciously, impressed.[25] There is a simple but typically classic utterance by Mr. Dooley on this theme. The difference between the attitude of the Supreme Court to New Deal legislation in the first term Mr. Roosevelt held office, and in his second, is a living part of

[25] See Fairman, *op. cit.*

our memories. But perhaps I may lay my emphasis on the utterance of a great English judge, Lord Justice Scrutton, a great lawyer, a powerful mind, and a great gentleman. He knew, as well as most, how the judge is affected by the environment in which he mostly moves from the early years of his call to the Bar. He assumed that the judge had no desire to be consciously powerful in his decisions. But, he added, "the habits you are trained in, the people with whom you mix, lead to your having a certain class of ideas of such a nature that, when you have to deal with other ideas, you do not give quite as sound and accurate judgments as you would wish." This is one of the great difficulties at present with labor. Labor says, "Where are your impartial judges? They all move in the same circle as the employers, they are all educated and nursed in the same ideas as the employers. How can a trade unionist or a labor man get impartial justice? It is very difficult somehow to be sure that you have put yourself into a thoroughly impartial position between two disputants, one of your own class and not one of your class." [26] I do not think that Lord Justice Scrutton was exaggerating the difficulties of which he wrote. The major assumption of the courts is that anti-competitive practices by the union ought to be prohibited, but that this should not interfere with " legitimate" union practices. I am not certain that most of the judges are sure, in this background, just what is meant, first, by "anti-competitive," and, second, by "legitimate." If they do know, I think they have concealed a good deal of their knowledge from the public view.

In fact, it is not very far from the truth to say that the courts approach the trade unions in a dual frame of mind. On the one hand, they see the unions as increasingly monopolistic barriers in the way of that free competition the prin-

[26] *Cambridge Law Journal* (1923).

ciples of the Common Law have been promoting for something like two centuries and a half. On the other hand, they are compelled to view them in the light of strategies which have given the unions a means of by-passing the obstacles the Common Law would have placed in their way. Most lawyers have a half-conscious belief that the Common Law provides, so to say, a law behind the law which is enacted by Parliament or Congress or a state legislature. There is amongst them a kind of nostalgia for the law as it stood before the New Deal legislation in the United States, and before the Trades Disputes Act of 1906 in Great Britain. They know that it is practically impossible to abrogate the right to strike in a democratic community. But they think that trade unions ought not to use their power "unreasonably." "Unreasonably" means different things to different courts. But, by and large, I think what it means is, (1) that the unions ought to respond to a request from the government to settle a dispute in any important industry by some means that will avoid any interruption in the service such an industry supplies; (2) that unions ought so to discipline their members that they do not embark upon "unofficial" strikes—that is, strikes which are not authorized by the appropriate organs of the union; (3) that unions ought, especially in important industries, to refrain from striking until their claims have been investigated by an independent body which has provided an impartial analysis about the facts upon the basis of which the union has made its claims and met with a refusal to which it replies with a threat to strike.

Mr. Thurman Arnold has gone further.[27] He would forbid the use of trade-union power to prevent the use of improved methods in business, new machinery, for example, or new

[27] Thurman Arnold, *The Bottlenecks of Business* (New York: Reynal & Hitchcock, 1940), pp. 250-52.

materials. He protests against those unions which compel an employer to hire unnecessary workers, in order to insure full employment for their members; in this conduct, of course, he draws powerful support from the practices of Mr. Petrillo and the musicians' union, as well as from the habits of the truckers' union in New York City.[28] He desires, thirdly, the prohibition of strikes which are intended only to further what in Great Britain we call "demarcation disputes," all too familiar to Americans as "jurisdictional disputes"; and he would include in these an attempt by a union to destroy some collective agreement between an employer and his workers in order to replace it with a new agreement under union patronage. There are some other types of union techniques Mr. Arnold would prohibit, but they are less important. To the practices he has condemned may be added certain others upon which the Supreme Court has frowned. The first is the type where the union forbids any of its members to work for a particular employer, even though the latter is willing to accept the terms the union normally makes with his competitors.[29] The second is where a union, or one of its branches, refuses to allow materials to be used which have not been manufactured by its own members.[30] Obviously this might easily be extended by the union over a very wide field. The House of Lords has held it illegal for a trade union, the members of which were paid on a sliding scale of wages adjusted to the price of coal in the market, to strike from time to time in order to make the coal relatively scarce, and by thus forcing up its price to consumers to get for themselves a higher rate of pay.[31] To these

[28] *U.S.* v. *Local 807*, 315 U.S. 521 (1902).

[29] *Hunt* v. *Cramboch*, 325 U.S. 821 (1945).

[30] *Allen Cradley Company* v. *Local No. 3*, 325 U.S. 197 (1945).

[31] *South Wales Miners' Federation* v. *Glamorgen Coal Company*, A.C. 239 (1905).

types of prohibition may be added the type that arises where unions compete with one another for the control of the employees of some firm, and the defeated union injures the firm by boycotting its other plants, or threatening to do so, unless it refuses to deal with the victorious union; this may be an important matter if the defeated union has been successful in obtaining control of those other plants, since the Supreme Court has held that the union certified by the National Labor Relations Board as the one that has won recognition is the one with which the employers must deal.[32] A firm which has a number of branches may then find that it is placed at a grave disadvantage by obeying a law which does not take account of its over-all position.

3

That there are important abuses in union practice which stand in serious need of correction I should not for one moment deny. But generally I am disturbed by the view that, unless there has been a plain breach of enacted law, the courts are the proper place in which to correct the abuses. In the absence of specific statutes the courts are dependent in Great Britain upon the implications of the Common Law, and in the United States upon these implications and upon those of the Constitution as well. Both these kinds of implications are political decisions; they are given by theories of public policy, which not only change from one period to another, but may also, in the same period, deeply divide a given court. It is, if I may venture to say so, pretty startling to a foreign observer to see the immense difference in approach toward even statutory change in President Roose-

[32] *Frank Brothers* v. *National Labor Relations Board,* 321 U.S. 702 (1944).

velt's first and second terms. I am not certain, further, that it is not still more startling to see the difference in approach after the reconstruction of the Supreme Court's personnel by President Roosevelt and President Truman. It is difficult not to feel that each judge tries to have his own view of the desirable limits within which the Court should make its interpretation of a case before it; and it is obvious that we have now ceased to accept the fiction that the judge finds the law, and does not make it, in the complex and delicate realm of trade-union activity. The smaller the area in which judge-made law decides between the lawful and the unlawful, the better for all concerned. Judicial invasion in this realm is more likely to bring the law into disrepute than in any other. That has been shown by both British and American experience. The distrust of the courts by the trade unions in Great Britain goes deep; and I add that it is by no means confined to the higher courts of law. Trade unions in the United States do not think very differently. Everyone knows that Mr. Justice Marshall's decision in the Marbury case was essentially a political act. So, too, was Mr. Justice Taney's decision in the Dred Scott case. I hardly need to remind you of Lincoln's famous attack upon the Supreme Court's action in that case, and his demand for its reversal lest the people be regarded as having "assigned this government into the hands of that eminent tribunal." If one compares the treatment received from the Court by three leaders of the Western Federation of Miners, Haywood, Moyer, and Pettibone, who were kidnaped under circumstances which make it very difficult not to suspect that the Governors of Idaho and Colorado were parties to the kidnaping [33]—treatment which Mr. Justice McKenna, the lone dissentient against the decision

---

[33] *Pettibone* v. *Nichols,* and *Moyer* v. *Nichols,* 203 U.S. 192 (1902).

to refuse a writ of habeas corpus, denounced in strong terms
—with the treatment of the Sugar Trust in 1896,[34] it becomes
difficult not to feel that the courts are too little aware of the
impact upon the successful corporation lawyer of his dependence upon the great business interests. "Petty judicial
interpretations," wrote J. B. Thayer, "have always been, are
now, and always will be, a very serious danger to the
country." [35] To that admirable remark I cannot refrain from
adding the classic warning of Mr. Justice Holmes. "It is a
misfortune," he said, "if a judge reads his conscious or unconscious sympathy with one side or the other prematurely
into the law, and forgets that what seems to him to be first
principles are believed by half his fellowmen to be wrong." [36]

It is this atmosphere that we must bear in mind when it
is urged that the courts should define what Frankfurter and
Greene [37] have termed "the allowable area of economic conflict," as well as the methods that are permitted when that
area is defined. In the Debs case, as they point out, the
Supreme Court had no difficulty in finding that it ought to
interfere in these matters by injunction. It considered this
power "one recognized from ancient times and by indubita-
ble authority." And they further point out [38] that this emphatic phrase describes what is in fact a power arrived at by
extending concepts originating in equitable jurisdiction over
nuisances. No doubt it is true that the affirmation of the injunction against Mr. Debs has its English analogies; but
there the injunction had a short life, whereas in the United

[34] 163 U.S. 437.

[35] James Bradley Thayer, *Legal Essays* (Cambridge: Harvard University
Press, 1927), pp. 158-59.

[36] Oliver Wendell Holmes, Jr., *Collected Legal Papers* (New York: Harcourt, Brace, 1920), p. 295. Speech of Feb. 15, 1913.

[37] Frankfurter and Greene, *op. cit.*, Chapter III.

[38] *Ibid.*, p. 20.

States it not only lasted nearly half the history of the Republic, but reached out to ever wider areas and aroused ever more bitter criticism. The more carefully, indeed, we look into the content of the words used in injunctions to prohibit such things as "threats," "coercion," "intimidation," and "conspiracy," the more skeptical we become that detachment is normal.[39] That was why Lord Justice Scrutton said that "I respectfully concur on this point with the admirable judgment of Holmes, in *Vegelahn* v. *Guntner,* where he remarks that the unlawfulness of 'threats' depends upon what you 'threaten,' and of 'compulsion' on how you compel. . . . The discussion of this question would be much more lucid if the disputants would observe certain simple rules—first, to avoid question-begging epithets such as 'boycotting,' 'ostracism,' 'the pillory,' 'coercion,' and the like; second, when they have used the word 'maliciously,' to say in what sense they use it. . . . Third, to have in mind the criticism of Garven, L. J., in the Hague case, approved by Lord Watson in *Allen* v. *Flood,* on the use of the words 'wrongfully,' 'injure,' 'maliciously.'"[40] It is not often, indeed, that, in the heat of a vigorously publicized dispute they are called upon to examine, the judges easily recognize that the extension of union action beyond the field of conflict between itself and the first firm it seeks to attack may make all the difference between trade-union welfare and trade-union destruction.[41] Yet the real truth is that until the Norris-La Guardia Act of 1932 American law in this field of economic conflict was transformed into the remedy of an injunction in equity, which has always been regarded as a special remedy for

[39] *Ibid.*, pp. 32-35.

[40] *Ibid.*, pp. 34, 160. The quotation is from Scrutton, L. J., in *Ware and Retread, Ltd.* v. *Motor Trade Association*, 3 K.B. 40 (1901).

[41] *Duplex Printing Press Company* v. *Deering*, 254 U.S. 443 (1921).

exceptional cases; and Mr. Justice Brandeis noted, with his
characteristic carefulness, that the injunction has for many
years "outshadowed in bitterness the question of the rela-
tive substantive right of the parties." [42] It may be true, as
Sir Henry Maine said, "that the progress of the law has been
secreted in the interstices of procedure"; it none the less remains the case that in few equitable cases have the substantive issues of the law seriously argued in a request for an
injunction. It is simply a swift and speedy way, with the
sanction of contempt at the disposal of the judge who grants
the indemnity, to offer to the successful applicant for its use
something akin to the sovereignty of the state. It embodies
that sovereignty in a single judge; and it leaves to him the
discretion to make a sanction for the infraction of that sovereignty, either by way of fine or imprisonment. The fine
may be staggering, as we saw recently in Judge Goldsborough's handling of Mr. John L. Lewis and the miners; and
the term of imprisonment may last for as long as twelve
months. Yet it is agreed by the main authority upon the subject that he knew "of no instance in which the witnesses
were examined orally in court upon a hearing involving the
issuance of a temporary injunction"; while Frankfurter and
Greene, writing some fifteen years later, were able to find
only seven instances in which there was an oral examination.[43] "Though the facts are crucial and the evidence supporting the facts the very pith of the cases, all we get are
affidavits and counter affidavits on either side; and some of
the former may be the work of the private detective hired by
the corporation to protect its interests." After the massive
evidence before the La Follette Committee on Civil Liber-

[42] *Truax* v. *Corrigan,* 257 U.S. 312 (1921).

[43] Frankfurter and Greene, *op. cit.,* pp. 68, 76. These are the experiences
of Dr. E. E. Witte, who made a special report for the U.S. Industrial Commission in 1915. Their decisive book was published fifteen years later.

ties, it is easy to understand why Frankfurter and Greene concluded that "to expect such a mode of hearing to elicit the truth about these ambiguous acts and motives of men is to look for miracles. To ask such a system of procedure to work without serious friction and without arousing wide skepticism regarding law's fair dealing is to subject the law to undue stress and strain." [44] They quote reasonably the question put by a New York judge: " 'Is it the law that a presumption of guilt attaches to a labor union association?' " The real fact simply is that when a court issued an injunction, in the great majority of cases it had already, without any real knowledge of the issue, brought down the strong hand of the state power insistently on one side. That was one of the reasons it was sought for by the employer. It created the impression that the law had already decided the issue against the strikers. No one will accuse Chief Justice Taft of a radical outlook; but he did not doubt that it had the result of discouraging men "from continuing what is their lawful right." [45]

It will doubtless be said that in examining an injunction I have exhumed a corpse; everyone now accepts as over and done with the age when the injunction was the primary weapon in trade-union disputes. But, apart from the fact that this has not been the case where the federal government has intervened since 1945, it is clear that the Supreme Court is once again moving toward that difficult borderline where, in its claim to protect society from the effect of methods it dislikes in conflicts between capital and labor, it is beginning to lay down standards of behavior in a way that reminds us of the pre-Roosevelt era. In the strange case of

[44] *Ibid.*, p. 78, especially n. 113.

[45] *Ibid.*, p. 80, n. 129. Chief Justice Taft made this speech in accepting the nomination as presidential candidate in 1908.

Wallace Corporation v. *National Labor Relations Board* [46]
it is certainly difficult not to feel that the majority of the
Court has made it the purpose of the Wagner Act to see that
an employer is responsible for any union to which a closed-
shop contract has been given. To an outside observer, it
seems plain that the objective of that Act was precisely to
prevent employers from using their power to interfere in the
internal life of unions. In the Hutcheson case it seems as
though the majority of the Supreme Court has held that the
Sherman Act does not apply to trade unions as long as these
do not combine with non-labor interests to secure victory.
But Mr. Justice Frankfurter, who wrote the ingenious and
helpful decision in the Hutcheson case,[47] wrote a powerful,
even angry, dissent in the United Brotherhod of Carpenters
and Joiners case.[48] Here the purpose of the prosecutor was
to prohibit trade unions and employers from conspiring to
create a monopoly which closes the market in the same territorial area from competition. But the dissent in this case
seems to permit exactly the growth of those monopolies by
trade union-employer agreement which the Sherman Act
was intended to prevent; and in the Hutcheson case, by
eight to one, the Court held that "Congress had never intended that unions could, consistent with the Sherman Act,
aid non-labor groups to create business monopolies, and to
control the marketing of goods and services." Nor is it comforting to note that the Illinois Supreme Court may be permitted to prevent by injunction the use of picketing in a
strike where violence in the past has reached so high a pitch
that the Illinois court might well believe that picketing will
involve violence in any future case; and it becomes less

[46] 323 U.S. 288 (1946).
[47] *U.S.* v. *Hutcheson,* 312 U.S. 219 (1941).
[48] *United Brotherhood of Carpenters and Joiners* v. *U.S.* (1947).

comforting still when it is held that picketing may be limited
"to the area of the industry within which a labor dispute
arises." [49] The confirmation of the Illinois decision has the
unhappy effect of making past violence control the future
right of a trade union to make use of a method that, in itself,
is entirely legal. Another case permits the use of one injunction outside the territorial area affected by the dispute. But
it is very difficult to see that this is a principle the application of which may be attempted with a serious approach to
objectivity. A corporation may well own two plants, one in
the State of Washington and one in the State of New York.
In Washington the relations between the corporation and
its employees may be entirely satisfactory; in New York they
may lead to a strike. How is the effective area of the dispute
to be defined? How, even more, is it to be defined if the
corporation against which its employees strike sells its commodities, for example, to department stores all over the cities
of the United States? Would an injunction be granted to
forbid the picketing of the department stores which refused
to discontinue the sale of the corporation's product, on the
ground that if the corporation had a single factory in Massachusetts, the "effective area" of the dispute cannot extend to
Chicago or to Des Moines or to San Francisco? Certainly, it
is not easy to see how that principle can be applied without
what looks very like a wholly delusive precision.

What is true of the Court in labor cases is not less true in
its relation to civil liberties and in its relation to the grave
procedural issues which protect the individual citizen in
matters where it is alleged that a crime has been committed
and sentence has followed. The application of the due process clause cannot permit, as Mr. Justice Frankfurter has said,
one approach where property is concerned and a different

[49] *Milk Wagon Drivers' Union* v. *Hendon Dairies*, 312 U.S. 287 (1941).

approach where the rights of citizens are in jeopardy. Few serious students would disagree with his view that "in neither case is our [the Court's] function comparable to that of a legislature, nor are we free to act as though we were a superlegislature. Judicial self-restraint is equally necessary whenever an exercise of political or legislative power is challenged." [50] But despite these wise words the Court, almost always with a majority variously composed, will make new legislation, or even invalidate congressional legislation, if it feels that the case before it is one in which judicial self-restraint becomes judicial abdication. It moves less easily than before 1936 to substitute its own experience for that of a legislature, whether state or federal; but, on the record, there can be no doubt that it clings resolutely to the doctrine of judicial supremacy. It uses its power today more for the protection of the rights of persons and groups of persons who live by the sale of their labor power; it is lacking in the enthusiasm of the Court over which Chief Justices like White and Taft and, at one stage, Hughes presided to make the rights of property primary in the community. But there is nothing which leads us to suppose that a drastic change in its composition, such as that which it fell to President Roosevelt to make, might not occur again, with a president in office, supported by a congressional majority, convinced that the primary purpose of the Constitution is the protection of property against attack from the power of numbers. It is, indeed, significant that in his famous dissent in the Gobitis case, Chief Justice Stone used words about the protection of minority rights against the crushing power of a majority which provide the road along which a differently composed Court could move without undue effort in that direction.[51]

[50] *Jones* v. *Opdike,* 316 U.S. 586 (1942).
[51] *Minersville School District* v. *Gobitis,* U.S. 580 (1940).

4

If we agree that the legal relationships of the trade unions in the modern community ought directly to be defined by legislation rather than inferred, especially at their margins, by the courts, we are driven back to the analysis of two major problems. The first is whether the impact of the trade unions upon the legislature should continue, as now, to be effected through a pressure group, or whether it is desirable to build a political party upon the basis of trade-union membership. I have already argued for the second of these choices. I am not unmindful of the difficulties. There is a division in the labor movement between the AFL and the CIO. There is the ominous danger that a labor party's effort will be weakened by racial and religious heterogeneity. There is the issue presented by the fact that such a party would have to work for a vast continent where sectional differences go deep and where even the existing national parties awaken a genuine interest among the voters only when there are national elections. Nor is it clear to many of the trade-union leaders, of both the AFL and the CIO, that there is any essential difference between their outlook and that of a progressive Republican, Senator Wayne Morse of Oregon, for example, or of a progressive Democrat, like President Roosevelt himself. Though some trade-union leaders are Communists, they are regarded as not less likely to be a source of trouble inside a mainly working-class party than they are already inside the trade-union movement. Unless they were firmly refused admission, they would do the same damage to a new workers' effort in politics as they did in 1948 to the effort of Mr. Henry Wallace to found a third party; and this might well have unfortunate repercussions upon the trade unions regarded as economic organizations only. A decision to form a party, moreover, might not only alienate the best elements among the farmers; it might also lead to a rush into its ranks of middle-class elements, especially the unstable "intellectuals," who might jeopardize the basically working-class leadership of the new organization. The empiricism of a pressure group, effectively deployed, still seems most likely to utilize the maximum strength of trade unions whose members are only beginning to think in political terms. And when the leaders look at the immense change in status and power the trade unions have won since 1933, a good many of them view with foreboding so great an innovation. They remain convinced that the real function of an American third party is a temporary one. It compels one or other of the existing parties to adjust itself to a new equilibrium; and success in that adjustment, on one side, drives the other party to a similar adjustment in its turn. A third party is an expedient of desperation, and it disappears when the crisis that has caused its emergence is over. So, for example, the Progressive parties of Theodore Roosevelt and R. M. La Follette gave a new perspective to the historic parties in the United States. But their real function, according to Professor Schlesinger, is to act "as a safeguard to the peaceful and orderly development of American society . . . ; when there is no occasion for secret conspiracy and underground plotting, minor parties became the safety-valve of social discontents"; and Professor Schlesinger has pointed out that "while there is no basic disagreement between the old parties as to theory of government," third parties, while rarely winning more than an occasional electoral vote, like La Follette in 1924, "have served a useful purpose in directing the attention of the people to great problems as yet unthought of, and accustoming them to the consideration of novel ideas of public policy." [52]

Professor Schlesinger was writing in the Coolidge era, when the "war to end wars" had been won and the overwhelming economic supremacy of the United States was about to emerge on a world-wide scale. Ahead for his country lay, first, the great depression, and, second, the World War of 1939–45 from the catastrophic effects of which only the United States was able, at least temporarily, to escape. But it escaped them when it had already passed the prospect of horizontal expansion, and its own future safety depended upon the abandonment of the easy isolationism it had hitherto enjoyed. After 1933 it looked out upon a different world. In the internal life of the American people the end of the frontier meant nationalism and centralization, the increasing dependence of the states upon the federal government, the growing movement of American federalism from a loose union to a tighter unity, as Dicey long before predicted. On the international side, the large-scale collapse of Europe and the difficult position of Asia made America unable to repudiate responsibilities a failure in which would leave both Europe and Asia to the control of communism, itself the inherent denial of what Americans call their "way of life." Internally, the older parties had to yield to the trade unions a status they would never have deemed possible under Coolidge or Hoover; externally, it became obvious that what could be saved of "Americanism" depended upon the acceptance of exactly those "entangling alliances" their statesmen had rejected so decisively from 1929 until Pearl Harbor, on December 7, 1941. With the acceptance of "entangling alliances" as unavoidable after Pearl Harbor, they

[52] A. M. Schlesinger, *New Viewpoints in American History* (New York: Macmillan, 1922), pp. 284-87.

were also accepting obligations to trade unions without the help of which their place in the international partnership they sought to build would be less and less possible. Their leadership meant, sooner or later, either an economic catastrophe, or a vertical expansion of production at home which made the historic foundations of "free enterprise" a mere phrase behind which could already be discovered the accepted characteristics of the traditional collectivist state. Sooner or later, then, both the Congress of the United States and its Supreme Court would have to adjust the categories of their activity to new principles. The definition of American democracy, even with its limited volume of public ownership, would have to satisfy the habits of workers through whom alone they could make those activities give reality to the process upon which their international position depended. Otherwise they would lose their leadership in international affairs by their inability to satisfy the growingly significant place of the trade unions in American national life.

Here it is important to note that neither party has been anxious to satisfy the demands formulated by the trade unions since 1933. They were driven some distance in that direction by the influence of Franklin Roosevelt before the famous "quarantine" speech at Chicago in 1937; though neither party followed with any eagerness along the road he defined. To get the Supreme Court to follow that road he had to attack it with a vigor hardly equaled since the Civil War, and, perhaps, hardly equaled since the days of Andrew Jackson. Once he was dead, the tempers of both parties revealed less the lessons they had learned from his leadership than their anxiety to "tame" their own professions to the desirability of returning to more ancient ways. It is true that in the election of 1948 Mr. Truman won a remarkable victory, almost as much against the leaders of his own party as against the Republicans. But it is far from clear how far the procedural limitations of the separation of powers will enable him, in the best of circumstances, to implement the pledges he gave to the trade unions. Whether he fails on that account, or whether his goodwill is destroyed either by depression at home or war abroad, it is also far from clear that he can make the Democratic party follow steadily on the path which, by brilliant leadership, his predecessor compelled it to tread. It is only too likely that the outcome—foreign repercussions apart—of a new American depression would be to make the trade unions its first victims; while a third world war would see the businessmen, once more, demand a halt in the progress of trade-union power as the price of their full cooperation. In either case, the trade unions would find that they had to save their status by self-reliance, and they could not hope to achieve that in the necessary degree unless they gathered goodwill about them and marched vigorously into the arena where politics are determined by men who act by themselves and not through intermediaries who are less interested in the results they achieve than in the power they get for their services. It was not really accident that in November 1948 no one really knew, in any concrete way, the program of the defeated candidate, and that, despite all the warnings of the professional quidnuncs of the Democratic party, President Truman won what seemed to almost all observers an impossible victory by the emphatic way in which he pledged his government to measures above all notable for the concreteness of their content.

That leads me to the second of the legal issues it will be imperative to decide in the next few years. Even observers who are friendly to trade unions are anxious to redefine their place in the state. I have listed earlier, for example, the

prohibitions which Mr. Thurman Arnold would impose upon
them. What is to be said of such prohibitions? Few people
will deny the validity of Mr. Arnold's claim that there should
be a power in any community to prevent trade-union action
from holding up inventions or to force upon an employer
the engagement of unnecessary labor in some of the truck-
ing unions of New York. Mr. Arnold himself would, no doubt,
agree that the prohibition of antisocial practices should apply equally to the capitalist as to the workers; and that the
definition of what an antisocial practice is should be left, in
the first instance at any rate, to a legislature and not to a
court. And since a number of antisocial practices in industry are technical matters, which need the kind of analysis
required, for example, from the experts of the Federal Trade
Commission before they issue a "cease and desist" order
against the manufacturer of some patent medicine, it is fair
to argue that after a legislature has laid down general principles it is probably more satisfactory to rely for their application upon an administrative tribunal that, after investigation, reports to the head of a government department
empowered to issue an order which might, or might not,
according to its character, require the approval of Parliament or Congress before it became final, than upon a court
of law which has no specialist knowledge in this field.

Apart from the fact that the establishment by the modern legislature of what is, broadly, a code of social behavior,
which both sides of industry must respect, makes it desirable
that the trade unions should be directly represented in that
legislature, and therefore move directly into political action,
the proposal raises other issues. If there are malpractices
on the union side which are to be regarded as offenses against
the community, there are malpractices on the employer's side
of immense importance. There is the suppression of inven-

tion; there are price-rings; there are trusts and cartels, some of them international in scope. There are the grave issues connected with the largely outmoded patent laws. There is the abuse of the interlocking directorate, and the immense complex of problems connected therewith. There are the issues, to which the work of Berle and Means [53] first drew attention so impressively, which arise from the separation of ownership and control in modern corporate enterprise. There are the financial problems connected with corporate reorganization, many of which are, as yet, quite outside the competence of the Securities and Exchange Commission. Anyone who reads the history of a great firm of corporation lawyers, or of a great investment banking house, finds it difficult to avoid the conclusion that he is watching the diplomatic agents of an important empire going into action; it becomes hard not to forget that they belong to the same professions as a lawyer in a small country town or the small banker before, at least in England, he was absorbed into one of the giant banks of our own time. Nor must we forget here the employers' side of racketeering, the use of labor spies, the hiring of private armies, their ability, so infrequently denied, to call upon the services of municipal and state police, of the National Guard, and of federal troops. Once a code of behavior is drawn up to protect the community from malpractice on either side, it is clear that the degree to which the legislature will have to make provision for industrial regulation will be far-reaching indeed. The more carefully the range of that regulation is examined, the less suitable it seems to be for control by a court of law. It seems

[53] A. A. Berle and G. C. Means, *The Modern Corporation and Private Property* (New York: Macmillan, 1933). The labor developments are admirably summarized in David Lynch, *The Concentration of Economic Power* (New York: Columbia University Press, 1946). It is regrettable that there are no comparable studies of the British situation.

far more likely to look as though it involved a basic change in industrial relationships in which it becomes, generally speaking, impossible to draw a line between the functions of management and the functions of the trade unions. To achieve a system of behavior which secures the results most likely to benefit the whole community ceases, from this angle, to be a matter for the employers and for them alone. It becomes conditional on winning the consent of the workers' representatives in the larger, and, often enough, of the workers themselves in the smaller, issues of policy and management. The alternative is endless friction and constant disputes of a kind with which courts of law are unsuited by their nature to deal. We have increasingly to accustom our minds to the realization that hunger and fear have ceased to be instruments of discipline upon which a democratic community may successfully rely. Or, at least, if it seeks a continued reliance upon them, it is no longer likely to remain a democracy. For constitutional government in industry is rapidly reaching the point where the alternative to it is despotism tempered by rebellion. Obviously, when we have moved so far, we have reached a point where the use of the courts to make policy would be, in the light of their traditions, an error of the largest magnitude. It is in other directions that the source of progress must be found.

IV. TRADE UNIONS AND DEMOCRACY

1

IN THE brief compass of this work, of course, I cannot hope even to skirt more than the fringes of the immense theme. But I think it is worth while to dwell, however shortly, upon the largest aspects of the changes we are witnessing, and to seek to be clear in our own minds about the significance of this scale. I emphasize this because however profound the recognition by Americans, employers and employees alike, of the growing interdependence of our civilization, however generous has been their attitude—and it has displayed a remarkable magnanimity—to aid in the recovery from the devastation of the war and the exhaustion of capital resources in practically the whole of Europe, I am still tempted to believe that the change in the spiritual character of Europe is neither everywhere nor wholly grasped by American observers of the European scene. I add that these changes are likely in the next generation to be greater still in Eastern Europe, the Middle East, and the Asiatic countries, and that I shall be surprised if, by the end of the twentieth century, we are not also seriously concerned with similar changes in the African continent. Already there are signs of a breakdown in the power and prestige of the Arab Federation, with its vestigial feudalism, and fifty years from now the racial doctrines of Dr. Malan and his Nationalist party in Africa, which seem to have won a temporary victory over the native Africans, may look like the worst blow ever struck at the chance of understanding between white and black in the Dominion where he seeks to apply his special philosophy.

I suggest that we are in the middle of a revolution as wide and deep as that of the Reformation or of the French Revolution in 1789. It is not a revolution caused by the two World Wars, though inevitably their material and psychological demands have greatly deepened its influence. Rather it is the revolution which lies at the root of the two wars, and has, for the time being, transferred, for a period that no one can foretell, the center of economic supremacy from Europe to the United States. It is, in Europe at least, a revolution which was completed in the minds of men long before it began to find expression in institutions. That also was true of the Reformation and the French Revolution. It is only between the two world wars that we began to see, at least partially, the character of the change and its proportions. It is, moreover, the case that, just as America was influenced, despite the difficulties of communication, by the events in France after 1789, so, with the immense improvement in the means of transport, it has meant that the United States could not avoid the influence of events after 1914. It was not only that it was compelled, by its own interests, to play a decisive part in the two world wars. It was also that, not seldom quite unconsciously, the modes of its thought were adjusted to ideas and purposes it seemed to be anxious to repudiate. It needs no special insight to insist that a new era in American history began in 1933, and that the old era of unfettered competition will not return unless the institutions of political democracy are overthrown by some catastrophic development. We may even go further and say that the area of American economic life in which public ownership, and the power of publicly regulated private ownership, is much larger than most Americans themselves are normally inclined to imagine. It is probable that the greatest of experiments in this field—the Tennessee Valley Authority—is only the prelude to further experiments of the kind. Though there are, no doubt, many individual businessmen who recognize that a new world is in the making, it is nevertheless still true that corporate enterprise is not yet convinced that this must be admitted. The Taft-Hartley Act was one example and instrument of this view, but it is far from the only one. And it points to a difference between the American and the European approaches to the problems of the new social order in which, as I believe, the attitude of the trade unions may now be of decisive significance.

Do not let us mistake the complexities which surround the historical process, especially at a critical moment like our own time, when one social order is painfully giving way to another. The factors involved are many. If I stress the economic factor as fundamental, I do not ignore the power which other factors—nationalism, religion, color, race, tradition—still unmistakably possess in shaping the character of social change; nor the degree to which these react upon, and are influenced by, the economic factor. I am aware also that no new synthesis can be effectively consolidated unless those who define it can put behind the definition the sanction of that ultimate ability to coerce which is embodied in the state power, and in the state power alone. All eras of decisive social change, moreover, have a character of confusion which makes all insight into their direction a very difficult matter. You can see that in the Reformation, in the English Civil Wars of the seventeenth century, in 1789, in 1848, in the United States after the Civil War, in Russia after the immense upheaval of 1917. The contemporary revolution is still more confused because it began first, and has gone deeper, in what were backward nations before 1917, so that the habits of mind in the advanced nations have not seldom worn the appearance, and sometimes have actually been, counterrevolutionary in character. If you will think for a moment of how the United States, until perhaps the eighties of the last century, seemed to most European observers a threat to the social order they approved; of how to Americans of eminence—Gouverneur Morris, Alexander Hamilton, Daniel Webster, in the first half-century of the Republic, William Graham Sumner, Grover Cleveland, Elihu Root, almost in our own time—the fear of the majority was the central principle in their thinking; you get a sense of the way in which the direction of events seems to cast a shadow over the hope that a reasonable social philosophy will emerge. Few things cause greater passion than the demand for a reassessment of values. The wars of religion, the fury which greeted the findings of Darwinism, the dark anger against Lenin and his associates in 1917, the emotions aroused by the New Deal of President Roosevelt, the intensity of the Kremlin's conviction today that Soviet Russia's allies of yesterday are its foes of tomorrow, are but a few examples of what occurs when the routine of social relations we accept as broadly valid is roughly challenged by men who think them outmoded.

An age of profound social change makes very strange bedfellows. Mr. Churchill expressed deep admiration for Mussolini; Neville Chamberlain and Generalissimo Stalin are at least alike in their woeful efforts to come to a *modus vivendi* with Hitler. A distinguished English Conservative politician had never a doubt that Hitler was wholly evil; but Mr. Amery also spoke in warm defense of Japanese imperialism in 1931. It is amazing to look back on the days only half a century ago when the leaders of the great craft trade unions in Great Britain looked upon the emergence of the "new Unionism," of which Ben Tillett, Tom Mann, and Will Thorne were the pioneers, as a great threat to the solidarity of the workers and on the demand of men like Keir Hardie for a labor party independent of the older political parties as a futile gesture only too likely to put the Conservatives permanently in power.

Perhaps I may be forgiven, as a stranger from Europe, if I say that during the period from Dunkerque to Pearl Harbor I found it curious to see Mr. Norman Thomas upon the same platform as Colonel Lindbergh; and that if I have understood the motives which led Mr. John L. Lewis to join with Mr. Hillman and Mr. Philip Murray, in walking out of the AFL to found the CIO, then I have the right to be bewildered by his decision not only to return, with his union, to the AFL, but also to spend some part of his tremendous energy in seeking to destroy the CIO. The underlying principles for which he had made so powerful an argument at the famous convention when no influence was greater than his in breaking the unity of the American labor movement are still valid in general outline.

We are in the midst of a crisis because, all over the world, there is a disproportion between the forces of production and the relations of production. The disproportion varies from community to community. But one can no more seriously doubt its reality today than he can doubt that he is watching the last phase of the struggle between decaying feudalism and modern techniques in the Middle East. Now all relations of production are the outcome of that system of ownership the legal consequences of which the government of a community protects by its use, in their support, of that supreme coercive authority we call the state power. Slowly over a good deal of Western civilization, though not over the whole of it, and over no part, let us note, of the Middle or of the Far East, the rising businessman found, first, that constitutional government was the most effective means to protect the position he had won; then, as a rule slowly, and with periods of set-back, he found that the arguments by which he rationalized his right to constitutional government compelled him to accept the obligation to base constitutional government upon a democratic foundation. He admitted the validity of democracy in the sphere of political institutions; to a large extent, especially in the New World, he admitted it in social relations. The one area from which the principle of democracy was excluded—from which, largely, it remains excluded—was the area of economic relations. Private property in the means of production still remains largely outside the province in which the simple decision of a majority in a political society, where universal suffrage exists and elections are free, can divert it to public ownership. It is a sacred category so far never successfully challenged except at the price of revolution.

The modern trade union is a necessary element in the developing process of democratic life. But it is important to be clear about the purposes for which it is necessary. A good many of its historic purposes are still fundamental. It is still urgent to fight for recognition, to secure decent standards of living, to prevent victimization and exploitation. I am not myself a believer in voluntary unionism. I see no reason to protect by law the individual worker who is unable or unwilling to join a union and prefers to make his private bargain with his employer. The closed shop seems to me a logical outcome of collective bargaining; if collective bargaining is to have any meaning, the worker cannot contract out of its consequences on private terms. The notion that a worker should be free to dispose as he will of his labor belongs to an era of individualism which has now no longer any historical meaning, and has had none since the rise of the factory system; and it follows that the terms upon which men work ought not to be fixed upon a basis which allows the employer to hold in his hands all the main powers in the contract of employment.

But it seems to me not less clear that, with the end of a laissez-faire society, there ought to be less emphasis upon those functions that only the past of our social order made union functions; and there are other functions that it is imperative for the unions to assume with a vigor far different from anything so far attempted. Most, if not all, of the benefits trade unions have been wont to offer their members as an inducement and protection seem to be largely obsolete; they are benefits which the government of any industrialized community can organize more effectively and more amply than the unions. The wider the range of the social services in the modern state, the more likely is this to be the case.

Nor am I convinced that the union is the proper organ for the provision of general educational services for its members; these, as I think, are in their nature services which at different levels the government of a community ought to provide. And this is true also of the major part, at any rate, of vocational training. The complications of the old apprenticeship system are the expression of a relatively small number of crafts in which it is easy to see that the "practical" training which the rules of the union could offer to a limited number of entrants normally gave them a skill not easily obtained in any other way, while at the same time it protected the fully trained member of the union from the hazards of unemployment.

But two considerations here are decisive. The first is that the precondition of the closed shop is the open entry; it would be unjust to permit the union to have the privilege of the first without imposing upon it the obligation to the second. A purely vocational education, moreover, not least one which is limited to workshop practice alone, is a narrowing thing. It rarely produces the really balanced mind. It does little to make the worker see beyond the narrow horizons of his job; and it fails to offer him the chance of seeing beyond the boundaries imposed upon most workers not engaged in supervisory or executive functions, since modern industrial technique not only tends to limit the number of highly skilled workers it requires, but to reduce the average worker to a routine semi-skilled job it is frequently possible to learn in a few weeks, or months at most, with the result that the personality of the worker is rarely called at all fully into play during his working hours.

I know, of course, that many trade unions have built up admirable educational schemes for their members; and that they find these schemes an important way of maintaining a spirit of unity, even a public spirit, among them. I admit, at once, that there is much to be said for this view. Yet, in general, it is clear that the number of trade unions with first-rate schemes of training is small, and that the number of members who take advantage of such facilities is smaller still. It is, moreover, the fact that much of the non-vocational training offered by trade unions is either an attempt to make up for defective education at school, or, alternatively, an inadequate substitute for the education which, at their best, the higher institutions of learning in a well-organized community ought to provide. I should, therefore, argue that as a general rule the training of workers in an industry ought to be a charge upon the industry itself. It ought to be voca-

tional in part only; and there should be no practical training
that is not properly proportioned to the theory which lies at
the back of the practice. Up to the early twenties, I should
like to see that supplemented by cultural education for a
minimum number of hours each year. After the early twenties, obviously, the worker must be left to decide for himself
whether or no he wishes to continue his training.

On this basis, I assume that we have passed the stage in
industrial development where a line is drawn, often sharply
drawn, between management and labor, and where it is outside the province of the workers, whether in a particular
factory or industry, to cooperate in the planning of industrial
development. On the contrary, I believe that the introduction of what we in Great Britain call Development Councils,
with appropriate sub-organs for the smaller units of industry, has now become an indispensable matter. It is to the
Development Council that I should assign education and
training of the workers in industry, making the unions in
that industry the representatives of the workers; and I should
seek in the plant, if it is large enough, or in a grouping of
plants, if that be more effective because of the numbers employed in a given unit, to build a trade-union committee
which works out in detail the application of the principles
agreed upon by the Development Council to a particular
plant or group of plants. There should be, as I see it, a rate
or tax chargeable upon the employers in each industry for
this purpose, and spent on workers' education, in all its
aspects, by the unions involved. It is important also to link
up the provision, especially on the technical side, which the
industry provides from its own resources with the established community educational services, as with the university and the school of technology. One of the important
things from the angle of the community is an educational

realism which this relation with industry makes possible; and, on the other side, the relation makes possible, I believe, a safeguard that the teaching offered is, within its general standards, and its contact with the development of new knowledge, prevented from the danger of degeneration into a purely routine effort at learning certain technical skills. I am not, I should like to add, unaware that in this regard the organized workers have a good deal to bring to academic life. Above all in economics and in history, there is everything to be said for making this contact as close as possible. You cannot write history with any pretense to social understanding unless you are aware, with a direct and sensitive apprehension, of the workers' experience. And I grow more convinced each year that economic theory, particularly when its basis is rooted in the postulation of equilibrium as its starting point, tends increasingly to become an exercise in logic, a closed system of deduction separated from a changing life outside the premises from which it starts, unless it is refreshed by the continuous exchange of ideas between the man of theory and the man of practice. Certainly, I doubt whether the body of doctrine—from Alfred Marshall through John Bates Clark and F. W. Taussig, down to that exciting moment when Keynes compelled economists all over the world to look into the foundations of their ideas—was not largely an excessively simple rationalization, or abstraction, of things as they stood in the twenty years or so after the Civil War. It was too easily accepted as adequate. It is an unhappy comment upon its outcome that it was, by and large, so certain that its foundations were secure, that the chief exponents of its virtues took them completely for granted. They failed, therefore, to see the immense problems they ought to have been investigating.

I hardly remember any outstanding academic economist

in the United States who foresaw the great depression. Until the time of Keynes, most British economists in those dreadful years between the two world wars had little or no insight into either the causes or the consequences of unemployment. I do not suggest that an insight into trade-union experiences would have cured all this. But it would at least have set the relations of theory to practice within a framework of assumptions that had a more effective reality about it. And it would have made us all far more aware than we have been of how small is the real body of material we have worked with in seeking to make social policy. Mostly we have not found the right answers because the experience within which we worked did not provide us with the capacity to ask the right questions.

2

In the next two or three generations it is increasingly likely that our economic system will be a planned system, and one in which the kind of private enterprise to which the nineteenth century pinned its fortunes will play an ever smaller part.

What is the place of the trade union in the planned economy? What ought to be the rights it can possibly claim? What ought to be its own internal relations? These are all questions which press ever more insistently upon us.

In Russia, and in the countries over which Russia's authority is directly predominant, it is obvious, as I have argued, that the trade union has ceased to be independent in its policy-making. It is an organ of the government, and the area within which it has freedom of movement is relatively small. The members cannot strike. They may, through their officials, make representations upon matters of great importance, like wages, like the efficiency of direction in a factory, like the length of the working week. They may be given, as in Soviet Russia, the task of administering social insurance, of organizing the educational life of the workers, and providing many of the institutions and opportunities through which they have access to a fuller social life. It is their business also to watch over the workers' safety, and to see that the responsible management has not only taken all reasonable precautions against danger, but is aware of means whereby those precautions can be improved.

I would not want, for a moment, to minimize the importance of these functions. On the contrary, I think they are of great importance, and ever more, as they are actually organized, they bring the union, in its representative capacity, into forms and degrees of cooperation with the management of industry that, in general, appear to be more advanced and more profound than is the case in any Western democracy, even in the nationalized industries of Western democracy.

It is, moreover, disturbing that we have not yet found the proper forms through which to associate the trade unions with the management of a nationalized industry in a way that makes their relation democratically effective. No serious observer could accept the demand of some trade unions to have the main director of a nationalized industry in their hands. It is also obviously unsatisfactory to select a few trade-union leaders for important executive posts in management when the ownership of an industry becomes public instead of private. Even more, it is unsatisfactory to accept men chosen by and responsible to the trade unions upon the committees of management; they then would be in a position where conflicting loyalties would gravely impair the clarity of the decisions they would have to take. It is also clear that in the very size of nationalized industries, especially in the light of their responsibility to the political government, may lie the source of those bureaucratic deformations which are among the outstanding dangers of large-scale enterprise. There is the insulation of distance between the ordinary worker and the men who make the ultimate decisions. There is the tendency to equate fairness with uniformity, which, almost always, results in excessive centralization. Complaints are handled too slowly, with the result that a difficulty which began by being small may end by assuming an importance out of all proportion to its real character. Far too much emphasis may be laid upon formalism, with all the psychological malaise which a faith in formalism usually involves. There may be far too much negotiation between the central committees of the trade unions involved and the central board of direction in the industry, with the result that the rank-and-file workers may feel as remote from the chance of influencing the settlements arrived at as they were when the industry was in private hands. Nor must we omit the possibility that the criteria of efficiency applied to the working of an industry in public hands may well need, on a number of grounds, to be quite different from those which apply to it when it is privately owned.

There is no more essential principle in sound administration than the rule that structure should follow function; it is therefore clear that there is no single pattern of organization that the managements of nationalized industries should follow, since their nature, the methods of operation, and the traditions inherited are all so different. But there are some rules which all experience goes to confirm, and where these rules bear directly upon democracy in the economic aspect of the worker's life, it is imperative that the management of an industry, especially a nationalized industry, shall not only accept them "in principle," but give practical expression to them in the daily life of the industry. The first rule is the desirability of the maximum amount of decentralization, both territorial and functional, with a chain of clear and direct responsibility in the hierarchy of management. The second is that where decisions affecting the workers are made, appropriate steps be taken, through adequate organs of consultation, to explain the decisions to the workers at every level, and to convince them that their views are seriously weighed before the decisions are given effect. The third is that the methods of promotion and dismissal shall be agreed upon with the workers, and that the latter be given the right to an explanation of how they are applied in any particular case when they ask an explanation. The fourth is that all industries shall have post-entry schemes of training, to give the workers the fullest opportunity of self-advancement, and that these schemes shall be formulated and operated jointly by workers and management. Related to this is, fifthly, the need for welfare schemes in which, again, joint operation is fundamental. It is important, sixthly, that industrial research, whether technological or related to the health, including the mental health, of the workers, shall be conducted in an atmosphere that makes the workers aware of what it involves for them, and that, as far as possible, elicits their direct cooperation and utilizes what is too often neglected—their fund of practical experience The seventh rule is the desirability, at reasonably frequent intervals, of joint conferences between management and workers at which each side has the opportunity to probe the mind of the other, and at which the management takes care both to give an over-all picture of its plans and to submit itself to questions and criticism about their nature. The last rule to which I would draw attention is the grave undesirability of placing in an executive position anyone, from a foreman to the managing director of a nationalized industry, whose acceptance of the validity of trade unionism is in doubt, or who seeks to operate the industry while convinced that its public ownership is undesirable on political grounds. In the second case, however distinguished his expertise in the technical field, it is far better to use him as a specialist to be consulted than to put him in charge of a team of men whose best efforts are likely to be adversely affected by his skepticism. It is just as mistaken to give such industrial experts power over men in mine or factory as it is to put a general who sees no hope of victory in charge of a military campaign.

I venture to add a brief word on the criteria of efficiency in a nationalized industry in Great Britain. Thus far the Labour government seems to have assumed that the test of good management is the ability to operate at a profit, and it has been profuse in explanations and apologies, as in the nationalized aviation system, where there is a loss at the end of the financial year; it has even been able to make many trade-union leaders accept this point of view.

This seems to me a mistaken approach. I do not think that every government-operated industry, nationalized on grounds of public interest, can be looked at from the same point of view. We have not nationalized the public health service to make a profit out of it, but out of the conviction that this is the best way to maintain the health of the nation at the highest possible level. We do not look for a profit from the national system of education; it would not otherwise be a system offered without cost to the nation's children. By analogy, it seems to me reasonable to examine the character of each nationalized industry to see whether the commodity it produces should or should not be sold at a profit. I can conceive, for example, that travel by air over long distances has implications of social value so high that it would be worth

while to run the service at a loss. The development of road
transport makes it more than possible that the railroads, both
for freight and passenger traffic, will not be able to compete
with the lorry and the motor bus; but it may well be legitimate, on social grounds, to keep railroad tariffs at a level
where they result in loss, in the same way as the Post Office
maintains the telegraph service even though this does not
pay. We ought not to deny the benefit of electricity or a
piped water supply to the inhabitants of rural areas on the
ground that the costs may jeopardize the power to make
profit from either service when in public hands. If this be
admitted, it then seems to me important to emphasize that
the power to make profit in a nationally owned industry cannot be the decisive factor in settling the conditions of labor
for the workers in such enterprises. That, in general, wages
and hours should be a function of output in the industry I am
not concerned to deny; but it is equally essential that there
should be a minimum standard of living and a maximum
number of working hours in the day, as well as an annual
holiday with pay, for all workers in the industry, even if the
result of conceding these means a subsidy to the industry
from the national exchequer.

I infer from this a further principle which it is the duty of
the trade unions to bring home to their members. Wage
claims, as a rule, are conceived in terms of a flat percentage
increase, with the result that the higher the worker's wage,
the greater the increase he receives if the claim is conceded.
More than that: if the relativity of wages is altered in an
industry by reason of an increase in the pay of the lower-
earning groups, union leaders are often forced by their members to put in claims on behalf of their members with higher
earnings in order to restore the previous relativity, and, almost invariably, it is argued that the denial of the new claims

will result in frustration and bad feeling with a consequent injury to morale and discipline. I regard this attitude as a legacy from the period when the trade unions were craft unions, little interested in the skilled, even the semi-skilled worker, and specialized in maintaining a highly intricate wage structure built on an historic hierarchy of skills that derived less from the craftsman's ability than from the power of this group within the union to limit the number of apprentices who could enter the group and thus learn its special technique. At any rate, it is today the main function of a trade union in a democracy generally, and in a nationalized industry within a democracy in particular, to educate its members to recognize that its first duty is to its members at the base of the industrial structure. When it asks better conditions for those above the minimum, it ought to be able to prove that there is increased output per man-hour, or an obvious increase in the worker's responsibilities in a particular trade, or a significant increase in the cost of living by which the workers are measurably affected. But, most of all, the trade unions must put a growing emphasis upon the importance of increased output per man-hour. That means a direct interest, on their part, in the conditions that make increased output possible, both technologically and psychologically; and this, in turn, will require, especially from trade-union leaders, a knowledge of the management and financial sides of industry, and a close scrutiny of what technical research is making possible there. Given the possibility, which we now possess, of maintaining full employment, the trade unions must play their full part in moving from the era of scarcity into the era of abundance. It is not unlikely that by playing their part in this march forward the trade unions may make an immeasurable contribution to the preservation of the democratic way of life.

The trade unions which operate in Soviet Russia have a special context of high importance. As they operate in a one-party state, the major officials, not merely of every trade union, not merely in one of the constituent nations of the Soviet union, but, still more, in an all-Russian trade-union organization, are likely to be members of the Communist party, and the policy of the union is pretty certain to be set within limits which the Communist party approves. No doubt it is true that a good official, not least the party member who is the real person in charge of the workers' side of a particular plant, or one of its sections, will see to it that the public opinion of those for whom he is responsible is fully reported to the authority above him in the party ranks. No doubt, also, he will act, much as a shop steward acts, to prevent any managerial folly from upsetting relations between management and workers. But, when all is said and done, the real center of discussion-making over the whole area of industry and agriculture is in the party and not in the trade union. The latter has an advisory function that may well be of great importance, but it cannot impose its advice without coming into conflict with the party, and thereby coming into conflict with the state power which the party really wields. And since, in the party, policy on all major matters is made from above and communicated to those below, the Russian trade union has influence but not power; it is, indeed, not unfair to argue that its influence, where this is likely to count, belongs to the officials of the unions and depends upon them for its chance of moving upward so as to play its part in the shaping of power. In the last resort, the ordinary worker has less chance of shaping his own destiny than a respected trade-union member in the average well-run workshop in Great Britain or the United States.

I am arguing, therefore, that while, under modern conditions, the worker ought not to contract out of his trade union, the union ought not to be an organization which is nothing more than the instrument of the state purpose, as it has become in an ever-greater degree in the one-party state. Protection of the workers' standard of life means trade-union independence; only where that genuinely exists as something the rank-and-file worker believes in is it likely that the real source of trade-union decision will be inside and not outside the membership.

The fact simply is that, given the concentration of power, as it is concentrated in a community like Russia, decisions are taken for the workers, and not by them.

It is not necessary to deny the remarkable achievements of Soviet Russia in order to insist that the will of the trade union is an inference made from above by those in whose hands power is concentrated rather than the growth of a common purpose from below, which, after discussion of experience at every level, becomes binding upon the leaders once the decision is made.

No doubt there are trade unions in the Western democracies which have surrendered union authority to one man or to a group of men; but they are the exception, and not the rule. And it is worth while adding, I think, that a union which lends itself in this way to the domination of one man or even a small group of men is failing to achieve one of the single most important functions of trade unionism—the training of its rank and file in the art of self-government. It is as dangerous in the United States or Great Britain as it is elsewhere for workers to feel that decision-making is not their function. The result is to make them inert and apathetic in one of the major realms where activity and alertness are the safeguards against their becoming mere adjuncts of the machine they serve. Centralized power is not less corrupting in the industrial than it is in the political sphere; and the trade-union member who accepts orders without scrutinizing them and relating them to his own experience may come very rapidly to find that he has lost his freedom not merely to act, but even to speak, at the very moment when that freedom is most valuable to him.

The trade-union member, in short, who leaves its problems to be thought about, still more, to be decided upon, by his fellow members or by his officials is defeating one of the primary purposes of trade unionism. That is even more the case in the immense unions of our own day than it was when they were relatively small organizations fighting for their existence. Some of the large mixed unions in Great Britain, for example, have lost much by the remoteness of that relation between the central executive committee and the mass of members, who do little but pay their dues and remain detached from all other activities for which the union is responsible. There is one great union, for example, which, by reason of this situation, has a membership half of which is unable to vote. Its general secretary was chosen at an election in which only thirty-five per cent of its members voted. It has branches so large that, if all the branch members were present, it would be physically impossible for discussion to take place. It has sections so extensive that the officials in charge of them are buried beneath a great mass of clerical and office work, which is fatal to any direct knowledge of what the members are thinking. The attendance at its branch meetings varies, in the normal way, from five or six per cent of the members to a maximum of some twenty per cent on a vital occasion.

The result is twofold, or, perhaps, threefold, in character, though most of the results are closely related to one another.

The first result is that a large proportion of its strikes are unofficial strikes, and the officials of the union have far too small a part in their settlement; indeed, it has not seldom been the case that the unofficial strike shows, with grave clarity, how much the officials of the union are out of touch with their members.

The second result is the growth of a system like that of the shop stewards in the British engineering industries—a system that is largely the outcome of failure in the relevant unions to adapt their structure to the changing conditions of the industry. It is, I think, exceptional for the district officials of unions in the engineering industries to have anything like the hold upon the workers that is won by an energetic convener of a shop-stewards' committee. I should agree that the cause of both these results is that most district officials have an area too large for them to cope with, and that they have too many outside duties, even, if I may say so, outside ambitions, to work at their major task with the appropriate intensity.

The third result presents us with one of the most complex trade-union problems of the present age; and one whose solution is by no means an easy one. It is the problem of the activities of members of the Communist party in the trade unions.

It is easy enough to see why, in France and in Italy, they have been able to win a dominating influence. In each case, they led the fight against collaboration with Hitler and Mussolini in the long years of resistance; and I think it ought to be said that they led it with a courage and a resolution that are beyond praise. But in Great Britain and in the United States the situation is very different. In the former the Communists are in a very small minority; out of over eight million trade unionists, there are not more than fifty thousand Communist party members at the outside; while in the United States I do not think the proportion is even as high. Yet there is no doubt of their influence. You may dislike the methods by which they acquire it. You may feel anger at the volume of intrigue, misrepresentation, and downright lying, above all, the smear tactics they do not hesitate to use. Yet, when the last criticism has been made of the Communists, I think it urgent to recognize that by far the largest part of their influence is due to their greater zeal, the continuity of their devotion to the purposes they seek to serve, and the faith they have in the over-all end to which they give so intense a devotion. At a branch meeting their record of attendance far surpasses that of non-communists. If there is a long, sometimes tiresome agenda, they can be relied upon to endure it when others, wearied by the fatigue of endless petty detail, decide to go home. If there is an election for an official, they do not bring forward half-a-dozen candidates; they are careful to arrange their candidatures so that the maximum votes for which they can hope are concentrated on a single person. They do not leave their members to find their way about trade-union work by the light of nature. The Communist in a trade union is not only the recipient of instructions he must carry out; he is carefully trained in the art of how best to carry out instructions. He knows that where grievance exists his business is to take the lead in exploiting it. He is constantly on the alert for the chance to discuss, to analyze, to explain. Where difficulties emerge reaching beyond the factory or mine where he works, he is not only told in detail the policy he must follow, but he becomes, as it were, the liaison officer in a line of contacts, each member of which is urging the same policy in the same way.

Let me add that, in Great Britain at any rate, I do not believe that Communists take the lead in fomenting disputes. Their method is rather, when a complaint arises, to throw all their energy onto the side of the workers, to be most insistent that the conflict shall be settled only when the grievance has been met. They thus get a reputation, especially among the more inexperienced trade unionists, for giving more energy than their rivals, especially their official rivals, to the workers who are fighting the management. When the fight is over the normal trade-union sentiment is to let its memory die a natural death. The Communist likes to keep its memory vivid. I have been told, with simple conviction, by a miner of long experience that the Communists can be relied upon, in a case of victimization at a pit, for example, to keep working harder at helping the miner involved than the lodge officials of the pit. I do not think that is true; but I think it is one of the results likely to follow from the Communists' determination to dramatize and exploit every situation in which they become involved.

While, therefore, I wholly agree with most of the criticisms made by the Trades Union Congress in Great Britain or by the leaders of the CIO in the United States of communistic tactics, this criticism does not go more than a little way to explain the volume of their influence in the trade unions. The fact still remains that the Communist party secures from its members an energetic loyalty that is far and away greater than anything the ordinary member of the rank and file is likely to display.

In my own view, it is utterly futile for trade-union leaders to complain that a branch has expressed views which its members do not in reality hold, if the resolution passed by the branch expresses the views of the members who actually attended; the problem for the leader is not why the resolution was passed, but why a sufficient number of those who did not believe in it were not willing to take the trouble to attend in order to see that it was defeated. If the election of Communists to official posts in the union is resented, I do not think that the Taft-Hartley Act is the best way to express that resentment; after a period, its main result will merely be to get men elected who are not known to be members of the Communist party.

Once a democratic organization begins by dividing its members into those with full rights and those with limited rights only, it faces the danger that it may become the image of what it seeks to destroy by using the very tactics it has attacked. A free society cannot use proscription as a normal method without ceasing to be a free society. And if proscription is pushed too far, it has the worst result of all—that of splitting the trade-union movement into factions, each of which is in grave peril of hating the other more than it hates the exploitation to which both are subject.

I have read most of the tales of woe about Communist infiltration into one or another of the unions. The main impression these tales make upon me is that they record the failure in leadership of men who have overwhelming majorities at their disposal and do not know how to bring their majorities into action. For the most part, I think that the explanation lies largely in the gap between the profession and practice of democracy in the habits of those leaders. It is no more use blaming the Communists for doing what they think it their duty to do than it is to blame the heretic for persisting in his heresy. It is necessary to go far deeper than denunciation and persecution if a real answer to Communist infiltration is to be found.

Above all, let me add, it is no use trying to segregate communism in the way that the Prime Minister of South Africa, Dr. Malan, is trying to segregate the Indians and the

Negroes in the territories of that Dominion. You cannot fight communism successfully by physical penalties of any kind, short of the literal extermination of all Communists. That has been shown so often, in so many kindred issues, that it ought by now to be a commonplace the truth of which there is no need to argue.

Communism is an idea born of a special historical movement; it expresses a part of the needs born of that movement with the same intensity as Christianity embodied the needs of the generation in which it was born. Do not let us forget that all the things said by the pagans of the early Christians were said by the Nazis of the Jews, and are being said by non-communists of the Communists, even, I remark, of the Russians and their satellites by the statesmen of the Atlantic Powers. I have no faith in the power of a negative approach, especially when its main weapons are invective and rhetoric, to overcome a positive idea. The trade-union leaders will not destroy Communists in their unions that way any more than the Roman emperors were able, from Nero to Diocletian, to destroy the early Christians. Their task is to change the conditions out of which communism has grown; and therewith to remember that in an age of revolution it is not enough to be content with the "inevitability of gradualness." Far too many trade-union leaders approach the problems of an age of revolution as though they were given geological time in which to solve them. There could be no error more profound. It is swiftness of adaptation, the courage to be audacious, the sense that we genuinely participate in great events which have in them the seeds of hope, that give us the power to deal with those communist methods with which it is difficult to be tolerant. Only by going forward with equal ardor and deeper foresight can we meet their challenge.

3

The need we all confront, not least among the trade unions, is to make democracy democratic. That is far more than a merely formal question; and it is far more than a question of leaving opportunities open of which men may take advantage if they so desire.

Democracy means participation. It is above all the sense not merely of being ruled by law and not by discretion, but also of making your own experience articulate in the shaping of the law by which you are ruled. It thus becomes urgent for union leaders to make sure that their members actively participate in the political life of their community at the local as well as at the national level; it is important, further, that they should play their full part within the trade union itself. This has become more rare than we like to admit. There is a danger of oligarchical bureaucratization in the trade unions which is full of risk to the thing which gives democracy its meaning and, therefore, its life.

I do not need to give examples. But I do need to say that there are trade unions in which the relation between the chief official and the rank and file is not very different from the relation between Hitler and the rank and file of his brown-shirt army. That is a bad relation even if it results in important gains to the mass membership.

A trade union needs discipline; but the last thing it needs, and the last thing it ought to accept, is an autocratic dictatorship imposed from above. The evidence is unmistakable that it leads to a Byzantinism as indefensible in the relationship of a trade union as it is in a vast political empire. It has, too, the evil result that, when the leader dies, or retires, or is dishonored, the contest for power that follows may do serious damage to the union itself.

Another reason lies in the battle that is shaping itself be-self before our eyes between the Communists and their opponents for the control of the workers' power. It becomes a dangerous thing when the disruption of working-class unity throws the emphasis of non-communist effort upon a concentration of its authority toward the negative drive of defeating the Communists as the major objective.

That turns too easily into the kind of quasi-alliance with capitalism that in England was implied in the Mond-Turner era after the general strike of 1926, and that in America was the real outcome of that curious National Civic Federation which, in its net effect, really took the minds of too many trade-union leaders away from the problems with which it is their function to concern themselves.

The unity of workers in their trade unions will be maintained only by making unions democratic, and democracy, I repeat, is participation in which the rank and file are not only told they matter, but are really aware that they do matter to their own leaders. Over a period, it is the employers, and not the workers, who gain by the disunity communism provokes. The way to defeat it is not by a semi-collaboration either with the government or with the employers, but by making the workers themselves combine to secure by their own acts the ends that achieve a democratic commonwealth.

As soon as that is said, two things become clear. The first is the paramount interest of the trade unions not merely in the efficiency of their own members, but also in the efficiency of management, executive as well as technical. It is impossible for the unions to accept an arbitrary line between their function and the employers' function. Too much is at

stake for the lives of men to depend upon decisions taken
without their knowledge, without regard to their well-being,
in the name of those rights of property which it is still one
of the main functions of the state power to safeguard. I
pointed out earlier how small has been the area yielded by
property even in the midst of the new social changes we are
witnessing. Only strong and united trade unions can convince the owners of property that they have more to lose by
conflict than by peaceful concession.

A divided trade unionism is an invitation to social conflict
in an age that requires large-scale adjustment in the relations
of production. I cannot avoid the fear that those workers'
leaders who invoke the aid of the employers, still more of
the state power, to block the infiltration of Communist influence are doing great damage to their own future and that
of their unions. They should rely on their own strength to
protect themselves; and their strength lies in the democ-
ratization of the unions. No collaboration will ever persuade
employers to give up the central keys of the citadel of economic power. Mr. Walter Reuther was denied access to the
accounts of the General Motors Corporation with which he
had to negotiate for the simple reason that once such access
begins, he could use the power of his union to make adjust-
ments, both of finance and of technology, to which the General Motors' empire is not prepared to submit. And it would
require a legislative authority not available to Mr. Reuther
to secure that submission. The purposes of trade unionism
can never be war on the economic battlefield alone. At every
critical point the struggle moves on to the political stage.

That, again, leads us back to the necessity of mobilizing
trade-union power politically so that it can carry out the
redefinition of the relations of production with the state
power in its hands, and not in its opponents' hands. This is

not an issue where a purely empirical approach is in dispute. The strategy and tactics of trade-union action in politics may be as empirical as you please; but it is not less essential that they should relate to a philosophy of history which recognizes, in the light of the record, that when the state power belongs to the owners of economic power—and it has always belonged to them—it will be used to define relations of production which benefit those owners.

This is not an attempt to make capitalists out as more evil than other men. It is not even an attempt to read American history in terms of the more rigid social structure of European states. It is not a denial that there is greater opportunity for the worker in America than in Europe, or that economic mobility is greater. I accept all these affirmations as true. I would even add to them many other traits—audacity, experimentalism, a refusal to submit to any predestined place in the social structure—all of which have marked American economic history in a far higher degree than is the case in Europe. I am asking you only to recognize the importance of realizing that the historical process is not a series of fortuitous occurrences but is capable of a rational explanation in causal terms.

I suggest that the degree to which man rationalizes his desires into principles of social and political action is the necessary starting point of any serious analysis of the human record. And once this is admitted, we have the clue from which the clear relationship between economic power and political forms can be inferred. It is obvious that democracy is, in a general way, of far more importance to the wage-earner than to any other section of the community.

Democracy as a form of political organization has always been limited in its power of fulfillment by the character of the relations of production, and these, in their turn, depend upon the way in which economic power is owned at any time. That the relation between economic power and political forms is influenced by other factors, religion, for instance, or national feeling, I do not seek for a moment to deny. I am merely posing the problem that Macaulay put to an American correspondent just a century ago, in a famous letter. He urged that we cannot be certain that the owners of property will see the relation of democracy to justice, or to freedom, or to equality, in just the same way as the masses; the well-being of the workers, vis à vis the owners of property, has always depended upon their organized strength, and the clarity of purpose which lies behind that organized strength. I see no immutability about democratic institutions, least of all in so critical a period as our own. If, therefore, they are defended by a union of capital and labor—organized employers and organized workers—against a union of extremists who are also workers, I doubt whether the union between employers and workers will last any longer than is necessary to destroy the extremists. In that period I do not doubt that the employers will make large concessions to their allies. But I have no confidence that they will continue the alliance after the extremists, the people they really fear, have been defeated. That, after all, is the history of the French Revolution of 1832, of 1848, of the February Revolution in the Russia of 1917. It is the history of the English Reform Act of 1832, and it is the history, as Jefferson and John Taylor of Caroline knew so well, of the early years of the American Republic.

It is to prevent the calamities which, in all the cases known to me, democracy has suffered when it has thrown property owners into a panic that I seek the two purposes I have here emphasized.

First, I think there must be internal democracy in the

trade unions; and, second, they must be able effectively to display their strength in the political arena. If there is serious weakness in either of these aspects, the whole structure of a democratic commonwealth would be in peril. And, to be quite frank, I think it is in real peril now. It is in less peril from the extreme Left than it is from those who want to destroy the extreme Left in order, so they say, to preserve democracy.

It was a great historian who said that you cannot destroy freedom abroad without ultimately destroying it at home. His aphorism has a wider application than he knew. The trade unions must be persuaded not to join in the destruction of their own extreme Left by mobilizing on their own behalf the authority of the employers and of the government. The result may well be—I think must be—very different from anything that we are led to expect. For the first outcome will be that the employers' side of the collaboration, having rid themselves of those they fear most, will be less inclined to yield to those who remain; and both the content and the pace of social progress will slow down. Since that will exacerbate those who know how immense are the changes we need if we are to develop our civilization rationally, the outcome will be the emergence of a new mob which will pose much the same kind of problem that the Communists now pose, but with more emotion and less reasoned insight. Nor is that all. In each stage of this process the government of a society not only becomes more accustomed to means of repression, but it makes progress in matters of social construction more difficult by accustoming men to expect repressions. Compare the ease with which President Roosevelt began the New Deal with the increasing difficulty he had in continuing it. Compare the fear of Russia in the United States in 1945 with the frenzied witch hunt that has been going on in the last two years. It does not require much historical insight to be aware that this type of witch hunt breeds fear. That fear breeds intolerance. The passion of them both, in combination, is fatal to our willingness to decide the problems we confront in terms of that persuasion by discussion which is the heart of constitutional democracy.

Let me conclude with a simple example. The trade unions of Great Britain have rarely rendered a greater service to mankind than when by their Councils of Action they compelled the Lloyd George government in 1920 to cease from intervention in Russia. The yearning to break the Bolshevik revolution was led by Mr. Churchill. There was no invective he denied himself, no sorry adventurer he was not eager to endow, in order to overthrow Lenin and his colleagues. What that crass error of judgment has cost us since 1920 is almost impossible to measure. The Russia of today is the outcome, in its fears, its aloofness, its haunting suspicion that even the offer of friendship is a form of conspiracy, of the movement against the Bolsheviks which no one did more than Mr. Churchill to turn into a European counterrevolution.[1]

I salute the proud record of leadership that is his in the war against Hitlerism. But I do not forget his ardor for Mussolini at one stage, or his hostility to the Spanish Republic at another. Salazar in Portugal, Horthy in Hungary, Metaxas in Greece, the royal dictatorship in Yugoslavia before the war—not one of these aroused anger in Mr. Churchill. Add to this his attitude to India,[2] and it is clear that the moving principle of Mr. Churchill's outlook has been less

[1] See Robert Sherwood's remarkable book, *Roosevelt and Hopkins* (New York: Harper, 1948), where the reader can see how this grim inheritance progressed until the eve of the Potsdam Conference.

[2] *Ibid.*, pp. 524-25.

the conscious and ceaseless will to broaden the basis of social justice than to safeguard with a minimum of change the social order in that British history in which he has played so illustrious a part.

And when, in 1949, I hear Mr. Churchill repeat all the ill-fated slogans of the First World War, and seek, not without success, the same ends as he sought a generation ago, my impulse is not to say that Mr. Churchill is engaged in safeguarding democracy from attack, but that he is seeking to re-create that coalition for counterrevolution he sought to build when Russia was weak. He is still trying, in the great name of freedom, to preserve a social and economic order which, at any rate in Europe, has stayed too long on the historical stage.

If we are able to reach a *modus vivendi* with those who, in the external field of relations, criticize our effort to settle our differences by discussion, I think that the future of independent trade unionism is safe. But if we should drift into the catastrophe of war, that attempt to secure freedom from aggression by a concerted alliance with those who seek to preserve the present social order may be fatal to the emancipation of men and women who live only by the sale of their labor, fatal, therefore, to the trade unions which seek to help them to make that sale under the best possible conditions.

That was the outcome of Ebert's alliance with the German forces of reaction after 1918; it was the outcome, also, of the fight in the Italian labor movement. It would in my judgment be the grossest possible error to think of Russia and of its supporters simply as nazism in a new national costume. If we do so, we merely play the game of those whose whole heart and interest is in the past. We are looking —how could we not look?—to a future in which the interest of the workers is the central base upon which we attempt to reconstruct our social order in terms of genuine justice and a freedom which begins to have meaning because it sets the welfare of the community above that of those whose whole title to authority is simply possession of economic power. The trade-union movement, more than any other movement, must beware of service to the historic maxim *Beati Possidentes.*

I am therefore led to the view that the trade-union movement, in a revolutionary age like our own, has a political task at least of equal importance to its economic function. No doubt it must seek, with all its power, to increase productivity; there is no other permanent way to advance the standard of life. No doubt, also, it is folly beyond defense to make demands anywhere in the realm of wages and hours, or in similar spheres, which can have no other outcome but to make inflation inevitable. It is one of the supreme duties of trade-union leadership to prevent what would be a catastrophic blow to the workers' hopes, since an uncontrolled inflation usually is paid for by working-class suffering.

Nor do I underestimate for one moment the duty of the trade-union leader to make the discipline of the rank-and-file members arise from their grasp of the situation, a duty, let me add, that calls for an intellectual grasp of the economic position which no government can ever of itself attain. And, beyond all this, it seems to me that the supreme duty of the trade unions in particular, and therefore of their leaders, is to set economic policy in the political perspective that makes its fulfillment possible. That political perspective is, at this hour, far more vital than any immediate, even if it be large, concession which leaves unchanged the present proportionate authority of workers and employers to define the ends for which the state power must be used.

I do not believe that this can be done by a policy of political collaboration. We in Britain tried that, under relatively fortunate circumstances in the two world wars.

In the first, the gains made in the war itself, as concessions to the workers, were more than lost in the lean years between the wars. After Labour entered Mr. Churchill's government in 1940—a necessary coalition—great changes were discussed in principle, but they got no further than discussion, owing to hostility from those economic forces which, in their political expression as the Conservative party, were those upon which Mr. Churchill chose mainly to rely.

When in 1945 the electorate gave to the Labour party that decisive majority to which, over nearly five years, the electorate has remained so remarkably faithful even in times of acute economic difficulty, the remedy proposed by Mr. Churchill and his party for our problems was a return to the policies of the interwar years, though the relatively smaller changes that seemed possible in the war years themselves both to him and to his followers now are obviously outmoded.

What saved Great Britain from social upheaval after 1945 was the fact that the government was in the hands of a political party built upon the strength of the organized workers and their allies; and there are few observers not aware that, were the forces of conservatism to regain the right to govern in the next period of British electoral history, constitutional democracy would be in serious jeopardy, for they seek to alter both the direction and the pace of social change. In such an institutional pattern the free trade union would have to struggle for its life.

In my view, therefore, it would be folly for the Labour government in Great Britain to accept criteria of values, and therefore the political policies which arise from them, from its opponents. These are set by the very forces which aim at replacing the Labour government on terms which would put the old values back. Those who would impose them would refuse to continue what the Labour government has begun, the serious attempt to redefine the relations of production by peaceful consent, and this in a way that preserves democracy and freedom. That is why we stand so clearly at the parting of the ways.

"The *enlightened* modern reformer," Professor Gilbert Murray has written, "if confronted with some ordinary complex of misery and unkindness, instinctively proposes to cure it by higher wages, better food, more comfort and leisure; to make people comfortable, and trust to their becoming good. The typical ancient reformer would appeal to us to care for none of these things (since riches notoriously do not make men virtuous), but with all our powers to pursue wisdom and righteousness, and the life of the spirit; to be good men, as we can be if we will, and to know that all else will follow." [3] The contrast Professor Murray has drawn so eloquently is hardly less true of the present time. The real task of trade unions is to refuse to accept the insistence that the contrast is permissible. None of us supposes that we can make a new world overnight. But all of us have learned that enough to eat, a decent wage, a comfortable house, health, and a leisure we have been taught to use in a creative way make self-respect far easier than when they are absent. That is why, after having been tried the world over, the kind of society in which the power wealth gives belongs not to the community, but is used by those chosen to rule it for the elevation of the few only, is found wanting. That the elevation of the many is an ancient dream does not make it less valid. It shows how deeply it has lain, historically, at

[3] Gilbert Murray, *Stoic, Christian and Humanist* (London: Watts, 1940).

the root of those yearnings which give each great age its character of achievement. The sin of man is to be satisfied with his past; his glory is to aim at a nobler future.

I do not deny that this aim involves social changes which are bound deeply to alter our lives, that the organized workers are called by their special situation to make the changes they need. I hope they can understand their mission with the clarity and resolution proportionate to the greatness of their task and act upon that insight. Action is imperative for the simple reason that we cannot stay still. Either we go forward to a community in which, as William Morris said, men share in the gain as well as the toil of living, a community, therefore, that is a fellowship of free men and women; or we move backward to a new and iron dark age.

My plea is the urgent one that trade unionists should understand their choice before it is too late; and, not least, that they should not mistake for the guardians of democracy those who have used the great name of freedom as a mask to cover their grim resolution at all costs to preserve their own power.

To choose the new world is a great adventure, in which the risks are many and the dangers great. But I think no other choice is open to a movement which has already moved so far toward the goal. Our movement has bred men of noble lives, passionate in their devotion, unresting in their effort, as energetic in their thought as they were prophetic in their vision. Our business is not to stand with those who, ever since its foundation, have sought the destruction of their effort. We are at the great moment of choice. We have to decide between the past, with its known limits of good and evil, and the future, with the joyous hazards of great adventure. We shall be judged by our steady courage in fulfilling the tradition our pioneers bequeathed us. They did not enter the promised land, even if they had some glimpse of its splendor. I do not know that we ourselves can hope to enter it, for we live in a hard and difficult time. But we do at least know how to continue the building of the highroad. It is in the resolution we bring to that task that we shall find the justification of the sacrifices we have exacted. Any other roads lead inevitably through betrayal to despair. Those who recognize that the workers must set the future of the next age can alone give its outline the perspective of genuine hope. We have reached a point where the enemies of labor can defeat its purposes only by the destruction of civilized life. Our task is to preserve that life for those who come after us, to deepen its promise, and to make men and women everywhere conscious that its promise is dependent upon peace.

Due